Global Warming: A Very Short Introduction

P9-DDS-501

© 2009

Newer edition, published in 2014
under title: _Climate Change:_
a very short introduction,
will be ordered in July 2019.
✓ Received.

VERY SHORT INTRODUCTIONS are for anyone wanting a stimulating and accessible way in to a new subject. They are written by experts, and have been published in more than 25 languages worldwide.

The series began in 1995, and now represents a wide variety of topics in history, philosophy, religion, science, and the humanities. Over the next few years it will grow to a library of around 200 volumes – a Very Short Introduction to everything from ancient Egypt and Indian philosophy to conceptual art and cosmology.

Very Short Introductions available now:

Available Soon:

For more information visit our websites
www.oup.com/uk/vsi
www.oup.com/us

Mark Maslin

GLOBAL WARMING

A Very Short Introduction

OXFORD
UNIVERSITY PRESS

OXFORD
UNIVERSITY PRESS

Great Clarendon Street, Oxford OX2 6DP

Oxford University Press is a department of the University of Oxford.
It furthers the University's objective of excellence in research, scholarship,
and education by publishing worldwide in

Oxford New York

Auckland Cape Town Dar es Salaam Hong Kong Karachi
Kuala Lumpur Madrid Melbourne Mexico City Nairobi
New Delhi Shanghai Taipei Toronto

With offices in

Argentina Austria Brazil Chile Czech Republic France Greece
Guatemala Hungary Italy Japan Poland Portugal Singapore
South Korea Switzerland Thailand Turkey Ukraine Vietnam

Oxford is a registered trade mark of Oxford University Press
in the UK and in certain other countries

Published in the United States
by Oxford University Press Inc., New York

British Library Cataloguing in Publication Data

Data available

Library of Congress Cataloging in Publication Data

Data available

ISBN 978-0-19-954824-8

1 3 5 7 9 10 8 6 4 2

Typeset by SPI Publisher Services, Pondicherry, India
Printed in Great Britain by
Ashford Colour Press Ltd, Gosport, Hampshire

Contents

To Chris Pace (1968–2006) and Nick Shackleton (1937–2006),
who never saw problems, only solutions.

Acknowledgements

The author would like to thank the following people: Johanna, Alexandra, and Abbie Maslin for being there; Marsha Filion and Emma Simmons for their excellent editing and the skill of finally extracting the first edition of this book from me, and James Thompson for persuading me to do a second edition; all the staff in the UCL Environment Institute, UCL Department of Geography, TippingPoint, and Cape Farewell; Cathy D'Alton and Miles Irving for excellent illustrations; Richard Betts and Eric Wolff for their insightful and extremely helpful reviews; and all my colleagues in climatology, palaeoclimatology, social science, economics, engineering, arts, and humanities who continue to strive to understand, predict, and mitigate our influence on climate.

Preface to Second Edition

The great thing I have been told about writing a preface is that no one reads it, so I can be as radical as I like. In my opinion, global warming is good for humanity. This may seem a very strange statement, so let me explain before you throw the book away in disgust. There are two major problems facing humanity in the 21st century: global poverty and global warming. Let's consider global poverty. At the moment we live in a world of plenty where 800 million people go to bed hungry and 15 million children starve to death each year. Fundamentally global poverty is about unequal distribution of global wealth and resources. To alleviate global poverty, we need to help poor countries to develop as quickly as possible. The golden rule of development is that it is always accompanied by an expansion of the amount of energy used. If these countries use the cheapest route, then their energy will be produced using carbon-based technologies such as coal, gas, and oil. For example, China is building a new coal-fired power station every four days. This of course will accelerate global warming. So to deal with global warming, we must deal with developing countries, and thus we must for the first time in humanity's history tackle the unequal distribution of global wealth. Hence global warming is making us face the forgotten billions of people on the planet, and we must make the world a fairer place. In the 21st century we must deal with both global poverty and global warming.

Abbreviations

AABW	Antarctic Bottom Water
AO	Arctic Oscillation
AOGCM	Atmosphere–Ocean General Circulation Model
AOSIS	Alliance of Small Island States
BINGO	Business and Industry Non-Governmental Organization
CDM	Clean Development Mechanism
CFCs	chlorofluorocarbons
COP	Conference of the Parties
ENGO	Environmental Non-Governmental Organization
ENSO	El Niño–Southern Oscillation
ETS	European Trading Scheme
GCM	General circulation model
GCR	galactic cosmic ray
GHCM	Global Historical Climate Network
IPCC	Intergovernmental Panel on Climate Change
JUSSCANNZ	Japan, USA, Switzerland, Canada, Australia, Norway, and New Zealand
MAT	marine air temperature
NADW	North Atlantic Deep Water
NAO	North Atlantic Oscillation
NGO	non-governmental organization
NRC	National Research Council (USA)
OECD	Organization for Economic Cooperation and Development
OPEC	Organization of Petroleum Exporting Countries
PETM	Palaeocene–Eocene Thermal Maximum

ppbv	parts per billion by volume
ppmv	parts per million by volume
SRES	Special Report on Emission Scenarios by the IPCC (2000)
SSS	sea-surface salinity
SST	sea-surface temperature
THC	thermohaline circulation
UNCTAD	United Nations Conference on Trade and Development
UNFCCC	United Nations Framework Convention on Climate Change
VBD	vector-borne disease

List of illustrations

The publisher and the author apologize for any errors or omissions in the above list. If contacted they will be pleased to rectify these at the earliest opportunity.

List of tables

Introduction

Global warming is the most important science issue of the 21st century, challenging the very structure of our global society. The problem is that global warming is not just a scientific concern, but encompasses economics, sociology, geopolitics, local politics, and individuals' choice of lifestyle. Global warming is caused by the massive increase of greenhouse gases, such as carbon dioxide, in the atmosphere, resulting from the burning of fossil fuels and deforestation. There is clear evidence that we have already elevated concentrations of atmospheric carbon dioxide to their highest level for the last half million years and perhaps even longer. Scientists believe that this is causing the Earth to warm faster than at any other time during, at the very least, the past 2,000 years. The most recent report by the Intergovernmental Panel on Climate Change (IPCC), amounting to nearly 3,000 pages of detailed review and analysis of published research, declares that the scientific uncertainties of global warming are essentially resolved. This report states that there is clear evidence for a 0.75°C rise in global temperatures and 22cm rise in sea level during the 20th century. The IPCC synthesis also predicts that global temperatures could rise further by between 1.1°C and 6.4°C by 2100, and sea level could rise by between 28cm and 79cm, more if the melting of Greenland and Antarctica accelerates. In addition, weather patterns will become less predictable and the occurrence of extreme climate events, such as storms, floods, heat waves, and droughts, will increase.

This book tries to unpick the controversies that surround the global warming hypothesis and hopefully provides an incentive to read more on the subject. It starts with an explanation of global warming and climate change, and this is followed by a review of how the global warming hypothesis was developed. The book examines the evidence showing that global warming is already occurring and the science behind the dramatic future predictions. The potentially devastating effects of global warming on human society, including drastic changes in health, agriculture, the economy, water resources, coastal regions, storms and other extreme climate events, and biodiversity, are evaluated. For each of these areas, scientists and social scientists have made estimates of the potential direct impacts and these are discussed.

There are also potential surprises that the global climate system might have in store for us, exacerbating future climate change. These include the very real possibility that Greenland and/or the Antarctic could melt, raising sea level by metres. Or the North Atlantic-driven deep-ocean circulation could change, producing extreme seasonal weather in Europe. There is the possibility of the Amazon rainforest burning in the future, accelerating global warming. Finally, there is a deadly threat lurking beneath the oceans: huge reserves of methane which could be released in 'giant burps of death' if the oceans warm up sufficiently – again, accelerating the warming of the planet.

The final chapters of the book look at global politics and possible solutions to global warming. The Stern Report in 2007 suggested that a global reduction in carbon emissions would cost about 1% of World Gross Domestic Product (GDP) to achieve, compared to the consequences, which could cost up to 20% of World GDP. This is a call to arms, shouting at us that we must quickly make the global economy more flexible and responsive to the challenge of a zero-carbon world economy. The last chapter provides a vision of what a zero-carbon world would look like.

In this book, I have tried to introduce the reader to the complexities of both the science and the politics of climate change. This is not a self-help, 'what can I do to make it better' book: if you want to alleviate your guilt, there are plenty of books out there for you. I am not against individuals taking concerted action to deal with global warming; rather, this book is about the large picture. I, however, believe the fundamental solutions to global warming will be at the global political and economic level. Global warming provides us with a unique opportunity to restructure global economics and at the same time provide a mechanism to alleviate poverty around the world. Current economic development is always accompanied by a massive expansion in a country's energy requirement. The cheapest way to meet this is through a carbon-based economy. So rapid industrial development and poverty alleviation lead to an acceleration in global warming. The twin problems of global warming and global poverty challenge our current concepts of the nation-state versus global responsibility. They challenge the short-term vision of our political leaders. Be under no illusion: if global warming is not taken seriously, we will all suffer, but of course it will be the poorest people in our global community who, as usual, suffer most.

Chapter 1
What is global warming?

The Earth's natural greenhouse

The temperature of the Earth is determined by the balance between the input from energy from the Sun and the reflection of some of this energy back into space. Certain atmospheric gases are critical to this temperature balance and are known as greenhouse gases. The energy received from the Sun is in the form of short-wave radiation, that is in the visible spectrum and ultraviolet radiation. On average, about one-third of this solar radiation that hits the Earth is reflected back to space. Of the remainder, some is absorbed by the atmosphere, but most is absorbed by the land and oceans. The Earth's surface becomes warm and as a result emits long-wave 'infrared' radiation. The greenhouse gases trap and re-emit some of this long-wave radiation, and warm the atmosphere. Naturally occurring greenhouse gases include water vapour, carbon dioxide, ozone, methane, and nitrous oxide, and together they create a natural greenhouse or blanket effect. Without this natural greenhouse effect, the Earth would be at least 35°C colder. Even though the greenhouse gases are often depicted in diagrams as one layer, to demonstrate their 'blanket effect', they are in fact mixed throughout the atmosphere (see Figure 1).

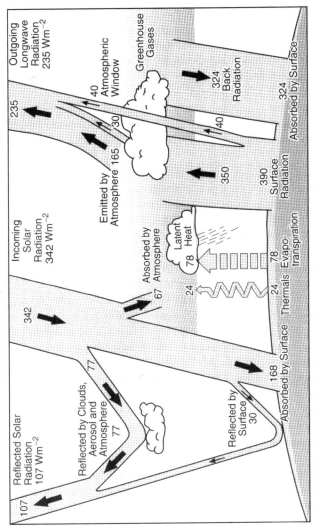

1. The Earth's annual global mean energy balance

Past climate and the role of carbon dioxide

One of the ways in which we know that atmospheric carbon dioxide is important in controlling global climate is through the study of our past climate. Over the last two and a half million years the Earth's climate has cycled between the great ice ages, with ice sheets over 3km thick over North America and Europe, to conditions that were even milder than they are today. These changes are extremely rapid if compared to other geological variations, such as the movement of continents around the globe, where we are looking at a time period of millions of years.

But how do we know about these massive ice ages and the role of carbon dioxide? The evidence mainly comes from ice cores drilled in both Antarctica and Greenland. As snow falls, it is light and fluffy and contains a lot of air. When this is slowly compacted to form ice, some of this air is trapped. By extracting these air bubbles trapped in the ancient ice, scientists can measure the percentage of greenhouse gases that were present in the past atmosphere. Scientists have drilled over two miles down into both the Greenland and Antarctic ice sheets, which has enabled them to reconstruct the amount of greenhouse gases that occurred in the atmosphere over the last half a million years. By examining the oxygen and hydrogen isotopes in the ice core, it is possible to estimate the temperature at which the ice was formed. The results are striking, as greenhouse gases such as atmospheric carbon dioxide (CO_2) and methane (CH_4) co-vary with temperatures over the last 650,000 years (see Figure 2). This strongly supports the idea that the carbon dioxide content in the atmosphere and global temperature are closely linked, that is, when CO_2 and CH_4 increase, the temperature is found to increase and vice versa. This is our greatest concern for future climate: if levels of greenhouse gases continue to rise, so will the temperature of our atmosphere. The study of past climate, as we will see throughout this book, provides many clues about what could happen in the future. One of the most worrying results from the study of ice cores, and lake

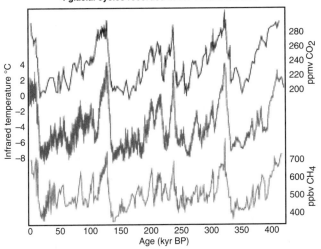

4 glacial cycles recorded in the Vostok ice core

2. **Greenhouse gases and temperature for the last four glacial cycles recorded in the Vostok ice core**

and deep-sea sediments, is that past climate has varied regionally by at least 5°C in a few decades, suggesting that climate follows a non-linear path. Hence we should expect sudden and dramatic surprises when greenhouse gas levels reach an as yet unknown trigger point in the future.

The rise in atmospheric carbon dioxide during the industrial period

One of the few claims of the global warming debate that seems to be universally accepted is that there is clear proof that levels of atmospheric carbon dioxide have been rising ever since the beginning of the industrial revolution. The first measurements of CO_2 concentrations in the atmosphere started in 1958 at an altitude of about 4,000 metres, on the summit of Mauna Loa mountain in Hawaii. The measurements were made here to be remote from local sources of pollution. What they have clearly shown is that atmospheric concentrations of CO_2 have increased every single year since 1958. The mean concentration of approximately 316 parts per million by volume (ppmv) in 1958 rose to approximately 379ppmv in 2005 (see Figure 3). The annual variations in the Mauna Loa observatory are mostly due to CO_2 uptake by growing plants. The uptake is highest in the northern hemisphere springtime; hence every spring there is a drop in atmospheric carbon dioxide which unfortunately does nothing to the overall trend towards ever higher values.

This carbon dioxide data from the Mauna Loa observatory can be combined with the detailed work on ice cores to produce a complete record of atmospheric carbon dioxide since the beginning of the industrial revolution. What this shows is that atmospheric CO_2 has increased from a pre-industrial concentration of about 280ppmv to nearly 380ppmv at present, which is an increase of 160 billion tonnes, representing an overall 30% increase. To put this increase into context, ice core evidence shows that over the last 650,000 years the natural change in atmospheric carbon dioxide has been between 180 and 300ppmv. The variation between warm and cold periods is about 80ppmv – almost the same as the CO_2 pollution that we have put into the atmosphere over the last 100 years. At the end of the last ice age, this carbon dioxide increase of 80ppmv was accompanied by a global warming of 6°C. Though the ultimate cause of the end of the last ice age was changes in the Earth's orbit around the Sun, scientists studying past climates have realized the central role atmospheric carbon dioxide has as a climate feedback translating these external variations into the waxing and waning of ice ages. It demonstrates that the level of pollution that we have already caused in one century is comparable to the natural variations which took thousands of years.

(a) Global atmospheric concentrations of three well mixed greenhouse gases

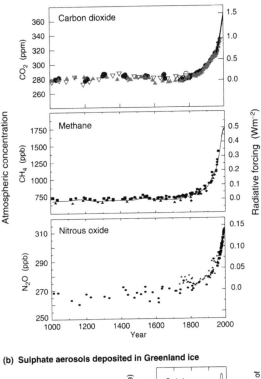

(b) Sulphate aerosols deposited in Greenland ice

3. Indicators of the human influence on the atmosphere composition during the industrial era

The enhanced greenhouse effect

The debate surrounding the global warming hypothesis is whether the additional greenhouse gases being added to the atmosphere will enhance the natural greenhouse effect. Global warming sceptics argue that though levels of carbon dioxide in the atmosphere are rising, this will not cause global warming, as either the effects are too small or there are other natural feedbacks which will counter major warming. Even if one takes the view of the majority of scientists and accepts that burning fossil fuels will cause warming, there is a different debate over exactly how much temperatures will increase. Then there is the discussion about whether global climate will respond in a linear manner to the extra greenhouse gases or whether there is a climate threshold waiting for us. These issues are tackled later in the book.

Who produces the pollution?

The United Nations Framework Convention on Climate Change was created to produce the first international agreement on reducing global greenhouse gas emissions. However, this task is not as simple as it first appears, as carbon dioxide emissions are not evenly produced by countries. The first major source of carbon dioxide is the burning of fossil fuels, since four-fifths of global carbon dioxide emissions comes from energy production, industrial processes, and transport. These are not evenly distributed around the world because of the unequal distribution of industry and wealth; North America, Europe, and Asia emit over 90% of the global industrially produced carbon dioxide (Figure 4a). Moreover, historically the developed nations have emitted much more than less-developed countries.

The second major source, accounting for one-fifth of global carbon dioxide emissions, is as a result of land-use changes. These emissions come primarily from the cutting down of forests for the purposes of agriculture, urbanization, or roads. When large areas of rainforests are cut down, the land often turns into less productive grassland with considerably reduced capacity for storing CO_2. Here the pattern of carbon dioxide emissions is different, with South America, Asia, and Africa being responsible for over 90% of present-day land-use change emissions (see Figure 4b). This raises important ethical issues because it is difficult to tell these countries to stop deforesting when historically this has already occurred in much of North America and Europe before the beginning of the 20th century. In terms of the amount of carbon dioxide released, industrial processes still significantly outweigh land-use changes.

So who are the bad guys in causing this increase in atmospheric carbon dioxide? Of course, it is the developed countries who historically have emitted most of the anthropogenic (man-made) greenhouse gases, as they have been emitting since the start of the industrial revolution in the latter half of the 18th century. But this is quickly becoming irrelevant because according to International Energy Authority projections, between 2000 and 2030 the world will emit more carbon dioxide in the atmosphere than between 1750 and 2000. This is because mature industrialized economies are energy-hungry and burn more and more fossil fuels. While less-developed countries are striving to increase their populations' standard of living, thereby also increasing their emissions of greenhouse gases at a huge rate, since economic development is closely associated with energy production. For example, China has now become the biggest emitter of carbon dioxide in the world, overtaking the USA in 2007. However, when considered per capita, the Chinese emissions are four times lower than those of the USA, who are top of the per capita list. So all the draft international agreements concerning cutting emissions since the Rio Earth Summit in 1992 have for moral reasons not included the developing world, as this is seen as an unfair brake on its

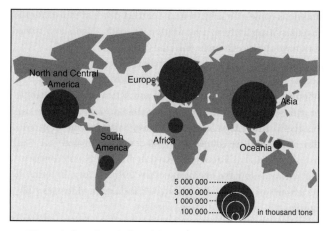

4a. CO$_2$ emissions from industrial processes

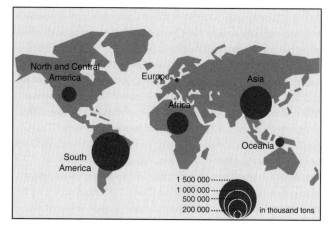

4b. CO$_2$ emissions from land-use change

economic development. However, as we will see later in this book, this is a significant issue because, for example, both China and India are rapidly industrializing, and with a combined population of over 2.3 billion people they will produce a huge amount of pollution. Therefore any agreement after 2012 will have to include the developing world.

What is the IPCC?

The Intergovernmental Panel on Climate Change (IPCC) was established in 1988 jointly by the United Nations Environmental Panel and World Meteorological Organization because of worries about the possibility of global warming. The purpose of the IPCC is the continued assessment of the state of knowledge on the various aspects of climate change, including scientific, environmental, and socioeconomic impacts and response strategies. The IPCC does not undertake independent scientific research, rather it brings together all key research published in the world and produces a consensus.

The IPCC is, thus, recognized as the most authoritative scientific and technical voice on climate change, and its assessments have had a profound influence on the negotiators of the United Nations Framework Convention on Climate Change (UNFCCC) and its Kyoto Protocol. The meetings in The Hague in November 2000 and in Bonn in July 2001 were the second and third attempts to ratify (i.e. to make legal) the Protocols laid out in Kyoto in 1998. Unfortunately, President Bush pulled the USA out of the negotiations in March 2001. However, 191 other countries recognized by the UN made history in July 2001 by agreeing the most far-reaching and comprehensive environmental treaty the world has ever seen. The Kyoto Protocol entered into force finally on 16 February 2005. It could only come into effect when Russia ratified the treaty, thereby meeting the requirement that at least 55 countries, representing 55% of the global emissions, signed up to it. In December 2007, the newly elected Labour Prime Minister Kevin Rudd of Australia signed the Kyoto Protocol, an act which was met with a standing ovation at the Bali meeting. As of April 2008, 178 countries out of a total of 192 recognized by the UN have ratified the treaty, leaving the USA as the only major country not to have signed up to Kyoto.

The IPCC is organized into three working groups plus a task force to calculate the amount of greenhouse gases produced by each country. Each of these four bodies has two co-chairmen (one from a developed and one from a developing country) and a technical support unit. Working Group I assesses the scientific aspects of the climate system and climate change; Working Group II addresses the vulnerability of human and natural systems to climate change, the negative and positive consequences of climate change, and options for adapting to them; and Working Group III assesses options for limiting greenhouse gas emissions and otherwise mitigating climate change, as well as economic issues. Hence the IPCC also provides governments with scientific, technical, and socioeconomic information relevant to evaluating the risks and to developing a response to global climate change. The latest reports from these three working groups were published in 2007, and approximately 400 experts from some 120 countries were directly involved in drafting, revising, and finalizing the IPCC reports, while another 2,500 experts participated in the review process. The IPCC authors are always nominated by governments and by international organizations, including non-governmental organizations. These reports are essential reading for anyone interested in global warming and are listed in the Further reading section at the end of the book. In 2008, the IPCC was jointly awarded, with Al Gore, the Noble Peace Prize, to acknowledge all the work the IPCC has done over the past 20 years.

The IPCC also compiles research on the main greenhouse gases: where they come from, and the current consensus concerning their warming potential (see below). The warming potential is calculated in comparison with carbon dioxide, which is allocated a warming potential of one. This way, the different greenhouse gases can be compared with each other relatively instead of in absolute terms. The global warming potential is calculated over both a 20- and 100-year period. This is because different greenhouse gases have different residence times in the atmosphere because of how long they take to break down or to be absorbed in the ocean or terrestrial biosphere. As you can see from Table 1, there are other greenhouse gases that are much more dangerous mass for mass than carbon dioxide and are much more effective at warming the atmosphere, but these exist in very low concentrations in the atmosphere, and therefore most of the debate concerning global warming still centres on the role and control of atmospheric carbon dioxide.

What is climate change?

Many scientists believe that the human-induced, or anthropogenic-enhanced, greenhouse effect will cause climate change in the near future. Even some of the global warming sceptics argue that though global warming may be a minor influence, natural climate change does occur on human timescales and we should be prepared to adapt to it. But what is climate change, and how does it occur? Climate change can manifest itself in a number of ways, for example changes in regional and global temperatures, changing rainfall patterns, expansion and contraction of ice sheets, and sea-level variations. These regional and global climate changes are responses to external and/or internal forcing mechanisms. An example of an internal forcing mechanism is the variations in the carbon dioxide content of the atmosphere modulating the greenhouse effect, while a good example of an external forcing mechanism is the long-term variations in the Earth's orbits around the Sun, which alter the regional distribution of solar radiation to the Earth. This is thought to cause the waxing and waning of the ice ages. So in terms of looking for the evidence for global warming and predicting the future, we need to take account of all the natural external and internal forcing mechanisms.

Table 1. Main greenhouse gases and their comparative ability to warm the atmosphere

Greenhouse gas	Chemical formula	Pre-industrial concentrations	2005 concentrations	Human source	Global warming potential		
					20 years	100 years	200 years
Carbon dioxide	CO_2	278 ppmv	379 ppmv (30% increase)	Fossil-fuel combustion Land-use changes Cement production	1	1	1
Methane	CH_4	700 ppbv	1774 ppbv (250% increase)	Fossil-fuels Rice paddies Waste dumps Livestock	72	25	7.6
Nitrous oxide	N_2O	275 ppbv	319 ppbv (15% increase)	Fertilizer Industrial processes Fossil-fuel combustion	289	298	153

CFC-12	CCl_2F_2	0.538 ppbv	O Does not exist naturally and is human generated	Liquid coolants/foams	11,000	10,900	5,200
HCFC-22	$CHClF_2$	0.169 ppbv	O Does not exist naturally and is human generated	Liquid coolants	5,160	1,810	549
Perfluoro methane PCF-14	CF_4	0.074 ppbv	O Does not exist naturally and is human generated	Production of aluminium	5,210	7,390	11,200
Sulphur hexa-fluoride	SF6	0.056 ppbv	O Does not exist naturally and is human generated	Dielectric fluid	16,300	22,800	32,600

ppmv = parts per million by volume
ppbv = parts per billion by volume

We can also try to abstract the way the global climate system responds to an internal or external forcing agent by examining different scenarios (see Figure 5). In these scenarios, I am assuming that there is only one forcing mechanism which is trying to change the global climate. What is important is how the global climate system will react to the mechanism. For example, is the relationship like a person trying to push a car up a hill which, strangely enough, produces very little response? Or is it more like a person pushing a car downhill, which, once the car starts to move, is very difficult to stop? There are four possible relationships, and this is the central question in the global warming debate – which is most applicable to the future?

(a) Linear and synchronous response (Figure 5a). In this case, the forcing produces a direct response in the climate system whose magnitude is in proportion to the forcing. In terms of global warming, an extra million tonnes of carbon dioxide would cause a certain predictable temperature increase. This can be equated to pushing a car along a flat road: most of the energy put into pushing is used to move the car forward.

(b) Muted or limited response (Figure 5b). In this case, the forcing may be strong, but the climate system is in some way buffered and therefore gives very little response. Many global warming sceptics and politicians argue that the climate system is insensitive to changes in atmospheric carbon dioxide so very little will happen in the future. This is the 'pushing the car up the hill' analogy: you can spend as much energy as you like trying to push the car, but it will not move very far.

(c) Delayed or non-linear response (Figure 5c). In this case, the climate system may have a slow response to the forcing thanks to being buffered in some way. After an initial period, the climate system responds to the forcing but in a non-linear way. This is a real possibility when it comes to global warming and why it is argued that only a small amount of warming has been observed over the last 100 years. This scenario can be equated to the car on

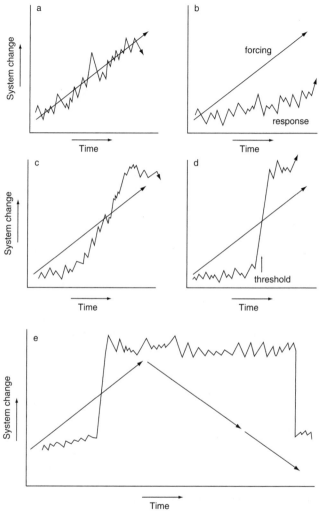

5. **Possible climate system responses to a linear-forcing**

the top of a hill: it takes some effort and thus time to push the car to the edge of the hill; this is the buffering effect. Once the car has reached the edge, it takes very little to push the car over, and then it accelerates down the hill with or without help. Once it reaches the bottom, the car then continues for some time, which is the overshoot, and then slows down of its own accord and settles into a new state.

(d) Threshold response (Figure 5d). In this case, initially, there is no or very little response in the climate system to the forcing; however, all the response takes place in a very short period of time in one large step or threshold. In many cases, the response may be much larger than one would expect from the size of the forcing and this can be referred to as a 'response overshoot'. This is the scenario that most worries scientists, as thresholds are very difficult to model and thus predict. However, thresholds have been found to be very common in the study of past climates, with rapid regional climate changes of over 5°C occurring within a few decades. This scenario equates to the bus hanging off the cliff at the end of the film *The Italian Job*; as long as there are only very small changes, nothing happens at all. However, a critical point (in this case weight) is reached and the bus (and the gold) plunge off the cliff into the ravine below.

Though these are purely theoretical models of how the global climate system can respond, they are important to keep in mind when reviewing the possible scenarios for future climate change. An added complication when assessing climate change is the possibility that climate thresholds contain bifurcations. This means the forcing required to go one way through the threshold is different from the reverse (see Figure 5e). This implies that once a climate threshold has occurred, it is a lot more difficult to reverse it. The bifurcation of the climate system has been inferred from ocean models which mimic the impact of fresh water in the North Atlantic ocean on the global deep-water circulation, and we will discuss this can of worms in great detail in Chapter 6.

Linking global warming with climate change

We have seen that there is clear evidence that greenhouse gas concentrations in the atmosphere have been rising since the industrial revolution in the 18th century. The current scientific consensus is that changes in greenhouse gas concentrations in the atmosphere do cause global temperature change. However, the biggest problem with the global warming hypothesis is understanding how sensitive the global climate is to increased levels of atmospheric carbon dioxide. Even if we establish this, predicting climate change is complex because it encompasses many different aspects which respond differently when the atmosphere warms up, including regional temperature changes, melting glaciers and ice sheets, relative sea-level change, precipitation changes, storm intensity and tracks, El Niño, and even ocean circulation. This linkage between global warming and climate change is further complicated by the fact that each part of the global climate system has different response times. For example, the atmosphere can respond to external or internal changes within a day, but the deep ocean may take decades to respond; while vegetation can alter its structure within a few weeks (e.g. change the amount of leaves), its composition (e.g. evolving plant types) can take up to a century to change. Then, add to this the possibility of natural forcing which may be cyclic; for example, there is good evidence that variations in solar output can affect climate over both a decadal and a century timescale.

There is also evidence that since the beginning of our present interglacial period, the last 10,000 years, there have been climatic coolings every 1,500 ±500 years, of which the Little Ice Age was the last. The Little Ice Age began in the 17th and ended in the 18th century and was characterized by a fall of 0.5–1°C in Greenland temperatures, significant shift in the currents around Iceland, and a sea-surface temperature fall of 4°C off the coast of West Africa, and 2°C off the Bermuda Rise, all of which were due to natural climate change. But interestingly enough, the Little Ice Age was a regional effect and does not show up on global records. So we need to disentangle natural climate variability from global warming. We need to understand how the different parts of the climate system interact, remembering that they all have different response times. We need to understand what sort of climatic change will be caused, and whether it will be gradual or catastrophic. We also need to understand how different regions of the world will be affected; for example, it is suggested that additional greenhouse gases will warm up the poles more than the tropics. All these themes concerning an understanding of the climate system and the difficulty of future climate prediction are returned to in Chapters 3 and 4.

So if you are reading this book for the first time and are primarily interested in the science of global warming, then I would suggest you read Chapters 3 to 6. However, I would encourage you also to read Chapters 2 and 7, which look at the social, historic, economic, and political aspects of global warming, since global warming, as far as I am concerned, cannot be seen solely as a scientific problem; rather, it is a problem for our global society. Then Chapter 8 concentrates on possible solutions for global warming and Chapter 9 is my vision of a zero-carbon world.

Chapter 2
A brief history of the global warming debate

Historical background

Scientists are predicting that global warming could warm the planet by between 1.1 and 6.4°C in the next 100 years, which economists suggest could cost as much as 20% of World GDP to deal with. In the face of such a threat, it is essential to understand the history of the global warming theory and the evidence that supports it. Below I will show that the whole debate over global warming clearly demonstrates how science is deeply influenced by society and vice versa. What we discover is that the essential science of global warming was carried out 50 years ago under the perceived necessity of geosciences during the Cold War, but it was not taken seriously as a theory until the late 1980s. I hope to give you some insight into why there was such a significant delay, and why global warming has now become one of the biggest political problems facing humanity.

It is now over 100 years since global warming was officially discovered. The pioneering work in 1896 by the Swedish scientist Svante Arrhenius, and the subsequent independent confirmation by Thomas Chamberlin, calculated that human activity could substantially warm the Earth by adding carbon dioxide to the atmosphere. This conclusion was the by-product of other research, its major aim being to offer a theory whereby decreased carbon dioxide would explain the causes of the great ice ages, a theory that still stands today but which had to wait until 1987 for the Antarctic Vostok ice-core results to confirm the pivotal role of atmospheric CO_2 in controlling past global climate. However, no one else took up the research topic, so both Arrhenius and Chamberlin turned to other challenges. This was because scientists at that time felt there were so many other influences on global climate, from sunspots to ocean circulation, that minor human influences were thought insignificant in comparison to the mighty forces of astronomy and geology. This idea was reinforced by research during the 1940s, which developed the theory that changes in the orbit of the Earth around the Sun controlled the waxing and waning of the great ice ages. A second line of argument was that because there is 50 times more carbon dioxide in the oceans than in the atmosphere, 'The sea acts as a vast equalizer': in other words, the ocean would mop up our pollution.

This dismissive view took its first blow when in the 1940s there was a significant improvement in infrared spectroscopy, the technique used to measure long-wave radiation. Up until the 1940s, experiments had shown that carbon dioxide did block the transmission of infrared 'long-wave' radiation of the sort given off by the Earth. However, the experiments showed there was very little change in this interception if the amount of carbon dioxide was doubled or halved. This meant that even small amounts of carbon dioxide could block radiation so thoroughly that adding more gas made very little difference. Moreover, water vapour, which is much more abundant than carbon dioxide, was found to block radiation in the same way and, therefore, was thought to be more important.

The Second World War saw a massive improvement in technology and the old measurements of carbon dioxide radiation interception were revisited. In the original experiments sea-level pressure was used, but it was found that at the rarefied upper atmosphere pressures the general absorption did not occur and, therefore, radiation was able to pass through the upper atmosphere and into space. This proved that increasing the amount of carbon dioxide did result in absorption of more radiation. Moreover, it was found that water vapour absorbed other types of radiation rather than carbon dioxide, and to compound it all, it was also discovered that the stratosphere, the upper atmosphere, was bone dry. This work was brought together in 1955 by the calculations of Gilbert Plass, who concluded that adding more carbon dioxide to the atmosphere would intercept more infrared radiation, preventing it being lost to space and thus warming the planet.

This still left the argument that the oceans would soak up the extra anthropogenically produced carbon dioxide. The first new evidence came in the 1950s and showed that the average lifetime of a carbon dioxide molecule in the atmosphere before it dissolved in the sea was about ten years. As the ocean overturning takes several hundreds of years, it was assumed the extra carbon dioxide would be safely locked in the oceans. But Roger Revelle, director of Scripps Institute of Oceanography in California, realized that it was necessary not only to know that a carbon dioxide molecule was absorbed after ten years but to ask what happened to it after that. Did it stay there or diffuse back into the atmosphere? How much extra CO_2 could the oceans hold? Revelle's calculations showed that the complexities of surface ocean chemistry are such that it returns much of the carbon dioxide that it absorbs. This was a great revelation, and showed that because of the peculiarities of ocean chemistry, the oceans would not be the complete sink for anthropogenic carbon dioxide that was first thought. This principle still holds true, although the exact amount of anthropogenic carbon dioxide taken up per year by the oceans is still in debate. It is thought to be about 2 gigatonnes, nearly one-third of the annual total anthropogenic production.

Charles Keeling, who was hired by Roger Revelle, produced the next important step forward in the global warming debate. In the late 1950s and early 1960s, Keeling used the most modern technology available to measure the concentration of atmospheric CO_2 in Antarctica and Mauna Loa. The resulting Keeling CO_2 curves have continued to climb ominously each year since the first measurement in 1958 and have become one of the major icons of global warming.

Cold War science

Spencer Weart, the director of the Center of History of Physics at the American Institute of Physics, contends that all the scientific facts about enhanced atmospheric CO_2 and potential global warming were assembled by the late 1950s to early 1960s. He argues that it was only due to the physical geosciences being favoured financially in the Cold War environment that so much of the fundamental work on global warming was completed. Gilbert Plass published an article in 1959 in *Scientific American* declaring that the world's temperature would rise by $3°C$ by the end of the century. The magazine editors published an accompanying photograph of coal smoke belching from factories and the caption read, 'Man upsets the balance of natural processes by adding billions of tons of carbon dioxide to the atmosphere each year.' This resembles thousands of magazine articles, television news items, and documentaries that we have all seen since the late 1980s. So why was there a delay between the science of global warming being accepted and in place in the late 1950s and early 1960s and the sudden realization of the true threat of global warming during the late 1980s?

Why the delay in recognizing global warming?

The key reasons for the delay in recognizing the global warming threat were, first, the power of the global mean temperature data set and, second, the need for the emergence of global environmental awareness. The global mean temperature data set is calculated using the land-air and sea-surface temperatures. From 1940 until the mid-1970s, the global temperature curve seems to have had a general downward trend. This provoked many scientists to discuss whether the Earth was entering the next great ice age. This fear developed in part because of increased awareness in the 1970s of how variable global climate had been in the past. The emerging subject of palaeoceanography (study of past oceans) demonstrated from deep-sea sediments that there were at least 32 glacial–interglacial (cold–warm) cycles in the last two and a half million years, not four as had been previously assumed. The time resolution of these studies was low, so that there was no possibility of estimating how quickly the ice ages came and went, only how regularly. It led many scientists and the media to ignore the scientific revelations of the 1950s and 1960s in favour of global cooling. As Ponte (1976) summarized:

> Since the 1940s the northern half of our planet has been cooling rapidly. Already the effect in the United States is the same as if every city had been picked up by giant hands and set down more than 100 miles closer to the North Pole. If the cooling continues, warned the National Academy of Sciences in 1975, we could possibly witness the beginning of the next Great Ice Age. Conceivably, some of us might live to see huge snow fields remaining year-round in northern regions of the United States and Europe. Probably, we would see mass global famine in our life times, perhaps even within a decade. Since 1970, half a million human beings in northern Africa and Asia have starved because of floods and droughts caused by the cooling climate.

It was not until the early 1980s, when the global annual mean temperature curve started to increase, that the global cooling scenario was questioned. By the late 1980s, the global annual mean temperature curve rose so steeply that all the dormant evidence from the late 1950s and 1960s was given prominence and the global warming theory was in full swing. What is intriguing is that some of the most vocal advocates for the global warming theory were also the ones responsible for creating concern over the impending ice age. In *The Genesis Strategy* in 1976, Stephen Schneider stressed that the global cooling trend had set in; he is now one of the leading proponents of global warming. In 1990, he stated that 'the rate of change [warming] is so fast that I don't hesitate to call that kind of change potentially catastrophic for ecosystems'.

Why the hysteria? John Gribbin (1989) describes the transition very neatly in his book *In Hothouse Earth: The Greenhouse Effect and Gaia*:

> In 1981 it was possible to stand back and take a leisurely look at the record from 1880 to 1980....In 1987, the figures were updated to 1985, chiefly for neatness of adding another half a decade to the records....But by early 1988, even one more year's worth of data justified another publication in April, just four months after the last 1987 measurements were made, pointing out the record-breaking warmth now being reached. Even there, Hansen [James Hansen, head of the NASA team studying global temperature trends] and Lebedeff were cautious about making the connection with the greenhouse effect, merely saying that this was 'a subject beyond the scope of this paper'. But in the four months it had taken to get the 1987 data in print, the world had changed again; just a few weeks later Hansen was telling the US Senate that the first five months of 1988 had been warmer than any comparable period since 1880, and the greenhouse effect was upon us.

James Hansen's case had been made stronger by the fact that in 1986, British scientists Wigley and Jones also succeeded in compiling 134 years of GMT data to show an unprecedented global warming trend starting in 1980, with the first three years being the warmest on the record. They had used different data and methods from other groups and thus served to increase

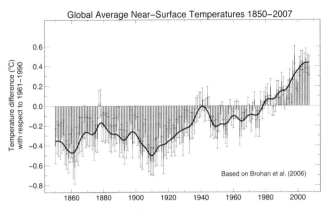

Global Average Near–Surface Temperatures 1850–2007

Based on Brohan et al. (2006)

6. Variation of the Earth's surface temperature

confidence within the scientific community that global warming
was underway.

It seems, therefore, that the whole global warming issue was
driven by the upturn in the global annual mean temperature
data set, the so-called 'hockey stick'. This in itself is interesting
because some scientists in the early 1990s still believed that this
was a flawed data set because: (1) many of the land monitoring
stations have subsequently been surrounded by urban areas,
thus increasing the temperature records because of the urban
heat island effect, (2) there have been changes in the ways
ships measure the sea-water temperature, (3) there was not
an adequate explanation for the cooling trend in the 1970s,
(4) satellite data did not show a warming trend from the 1970s to
the 1990s, and (5) the global warming models have overestimated
the warming that should have occurred in the northern
hemisphere over the last 100 years. Since the early 1990s, the
urban heat island and variations in sea-temperature
measurements have been taken into account. We now know that
the cooling trend of the 1960s and 1970s is due to the decadal
influence of the sunspot cycle and that pollutants, such as sulphur

dioxide aerosols, cooled the industrial regions of the globe. In addition, the satellite results were spurious for a number of reasons, and a greater understanding of the system and recalibrated data show a significant warming trend. So the latest IPCC 2007 Science Report has reviewed and synthesized a wide range of data sets and shows that, essentially, the trend in the temperature data is correct, and that this warming trend has continued unstopped until the present day (see Figure 6). In fact, we know that 1998 and 2005 were globally the warmest years on record. The temperatures for these two years are so close that scientists are divided on which is the warmest. However, 1998 was an El Niño year, which we know adds up to $1°C$ on the average global temperatures. So we can say 2005 was the warmest normal year on record, with 2002, 2003, and 2004 respectively third, fourth, and fifth warmest. Indeed, the 12 warmest years on record have all occurred in the last 13 years. While a mild El Niño ensured that 2007 was the eighth warmest year on record.

The upturn in the global annual mean temperature data was not the sole reason for the appearance of the global warming issue. In the late 1970s and 1980s, there were significant advances in global climate modelling and a marked improvement in our understanding of past climates. Developments in general circulation models (GCMs) during this period included taking into account the role of particles and clouds in affecting the global climate. Despite the cooling effect thought to be associated with particle pollution, the new ocean–atmosphere coupled GCM tools emerged with revised and higher estimates of the warming that would be associated with a doubling of CO_2 in the atmosphere. By the 1980s, scientific concern had emerged about CH_4 and other non-CO_2 greenhouse gases as well as the role of the oceans as a carrier of heat. GCMs continued to improve, and the numbers of scientific teams working on such models increased over the 1980s and the 1990s. In 1992, a first overall comparison of results from

14 GCMs was undertaken; the results were all in rough overall agreement, confirming the prediction of global warming.

In terms of the study of palaeoclimate, during the 1980s there was also an intense drive to understand how and why past climate changed. Major advances were made in obtaining high-resolution past climate records from deep-sea sediments and ice cores. It was, thus, realized that glacial periods, or ice ages, take tens of thousands of years to occur, primarily because ice sheets are very slow to build up and are naturally unstable. In contrast, the transition to a warmer period, or interglacial, such as the present, is geologically very quick, in the order of a couple of thousand years. This is because once the ice sheets start to melt, there are a number of positive feedbacks that accelerate the process, such as sea-level rise which can undercut and destroy large ice sheets. The realization occurred in the palaeoclimate community that global warming is much easier and more rapid than cooling. It also put to rest the myth of the next impending ice age. As the glacial–interglacial periods of the last two and half million years have been shown to be forced by the changes in the orbit of the Earth around the Sun, it would be possible to predict when the next glacial period will begin, if there were no anthropogenic effects involved. According to the model predictions by Berger and Loutre (2002) at the Université Catholique de Louvain in Belgium, we do not need to worry about another ice age for at least 5,000 years. Indeed, if their model is correct and atmospheric carbon dioxide concentrations double, then global warming would postpone the next ice age for another 45,000 years. Palaeoclimate work has also provided us with worrying insights into how the climate system works. Recent work on the ice cores and deep-sea sediments demonstrate that at least regional climate changes of 5°C can occur in a matter of decades. This work on reconstructing past climate seems to demonstrate that the global climate system is not benign but highly dynamic and prone to rapid changes.

The rise of the environmental social movement

The next change that occurred during the 1980s was a massive grass-roots expansion in the environmental movement, particularly in the USA, Canada, and the UK, partly as a backlash against the right-wing governments of the 1980s and the expansion of the consumer economy, and partly because of the increasing number of environment-related stories in the media. This heralded a new era of global environmental awareness and transnational NGOs (non-governmental organizations). The roots of this growing environmental awareness can be traced back to a number of key markers: these include the publication of Rachel Carson's *Silent Spring* in 1962; the image of Earth seen from the Moon in 1969; the Club of Rome's 1972 report on *Limits to Growth*; the Three Mile Island nuclear reactor accident in 1979, and the nuclear accident at Chernobyl in 1986; and the Exxon Valdez oil spillage in 1989. But these environmental problems were all regional in effect, limited geographically to the specific area in which they occurred.

It was the discovery in 1985 by the British Antarctic Survey of depletion of ozone over Antarctica which demonstrated the global connectivity of our environment. The ozone 'hole' also had a tangible international cause, the use of chlorofluorocarbons (CFCs), which led to a whole new area of politics, the international management of the environment. There followed a set of key agreements: the 1985 Vienna Convention for the Protection of the Ozone Layer; the 1987 Montreal Protocol on Substances that Deplete the Ozone Layer; and the 1990 London and 1992 Copenhagen Adjustments and Amendments to the Protocol. These have been held up as examples of successful environmental diplomacy. Climate change has had a slower development in international politics and far less has been achieved in terms of regulation and implementation. This is, at its most simplistic level, because of the great inherent uncertainties of the science and the greater economic costs involved.

Global warming and the media

The other reason for the acceptance of the global warming hypothesis was the intense media interest throughout the late 1980s and 1990s. This is because the global warming hypothesis was perfect for the media: a dramatic story about the end of the world as we know it, with significant controversy about whether it was even true. Anabela Carvalho, now at the University of Minho (Braga, Portugal), has undertaken a fascinating study of the British quality (broadsheet) press coverage of the global warming issue between 1985 and 1997. She concentrated particularly on the *The Guardian* and *The Times*, and found throughout this period that they promoted very different worldviews. Interestingly, despite their differing views, the number of articles published per year by the British quality papers followed a similar pattern and peaked when key IPCC reports were published or international conferences on climate change were held (see Figure 7). But it is the nature of these articles that shows how the global warming debate was constructed in the media. From the late 1980s, *The Times*, which published most articles on global warming in 1989, 1990, and 1992, cast doubt on the claims of climate change. There was a recurrent attempt to promote mistrust in science, through strategies of generalization, of disagreement within the scientific community, and, most importantly, discrediting scientists and scientific institutions. A very similar viewpoint was taken by the majority of the American media throughout much of the 1990s. In fact, it has been claimed that this approach in the American media has led to a barrier between scientists and the public in the USA.

In the UK, *The Guardian* newspaper took the opposite approach to that of *The Times*. Although *The Guardian* gave space to the technical side of the debate, it soon started to discuss scientific claims in the wider context. As scientific uncertainty regarding the enhanced greenhouse effect decreased during the 1990s, *The Guardian* coherently advanced a strategy of building confidence

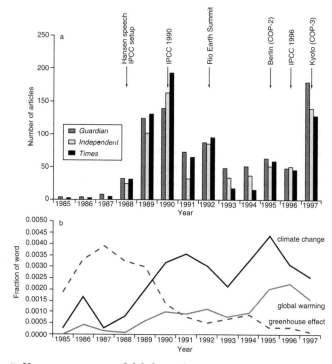

7. Newspaper coverage of global warming 1985–1997

in science, with an emphasis on consensus as a means of enhancing the reliability of knowledge. This was because *The Guardian* understood and promoted one of the fundamental bases of science, which is that a theory, such as global warming, can only be accepted or rejected by the weight of evidence. So, as evidence from many different areas of science continues to support the theory of global warming, so correspondingly our confidence in the theory should increase. Far from painting science as 'pure' or 'correct', instead *The Guardian* politicized it to demonstrate the bias that is inherent in all science. This clearly showed that many of the climate change claims were being eroded by lobbying pressure, mainly associated with the fossil-fuel industry. This politicizing of science allowed *The Guardian* to strengthen its readers' confidence in science.

Moreover, *The Guardian* clearly conveyed the uncertainties within the science of global warming, and the paper's editors were, and still are, in favour of the precautionary principle. It was through this media filter that scientists attempted to advance their particular global warming view, by either making claims for more research or promoting certain political options. From the late 1980s onwards, scientists became very adept at staging their media performances, and it is clear that the general acceptance of the global warming hypothesis is in part due to their continued efforts to communicate their findings. Indeed, both the sceptical and the supportive stances of *The Times* and *The Guardian*, respectively, so legitimized the debate over global warming that the public became aware that this was not an overnight news story but something that was to become part of the very fabric of our society.

It seems that the media has also influenced our use of words. From 1988 onwards, the use of the phrases 'global warming' and 'climate change' gained support, while 'greenhouse effect' lost its appeal and by 1997 was rarely mentioned. The change in terminology is reflected in this book. The title is *Global Warming*, as everyone knows what that means, and the major discussions in this book are about the climate change it might induce.

As mentioned, in the USA media coverage has been different. First, until recently there has been no pro-global warming media coverage equivalent to that delivered by *The Guardian*. Second, climate change sceptics have been very strong on using the media in the USA. For example, McInytre and McKitrick in 2003 attacked the global mean temperature 'hockey stick' by raising questions about the quality of data and accuracy of methods used to estimate trends in GMT. This debate has taken place between experts but in an unusually public manner. For example, one US scientist, Michael Mann, who has widely published on global mean temperature trends, has been the centre of the criticism and active in responding to it. Despite Mann's strong rebuttal and the weight of scientific evidence that brings into doubt the validity of the critique, both the media and US and British politicians have continued to bring attention to the questions raised by McInytre and McKitrick.

There are two possible explanations for this extraordinarily media-facilitated public scientific debate. First, political sceptics who do not want to see political action to address climate change may be using this debate about methods and scientific uncertainty as a convenient hook on which to hang their case for delay. The global mean temperature curve over the last millennium is a particularly important target for such criticism, owing to its emblematic role in the policy debate. Second, the media's ethical commitment to balanced reporting may unwittingly provide unwarranted attention to critical views, even if they are marginal and outside the realm of what is normally considered 'good' science. In the UK, *The Guardian* opened up the critical coverage by examining the motivations behind the science, thus providing the contested space within which reporting takes place. This, however, did not occur in the US or elsewhere in the world until very recently. The McInytre and McKitrick case thus demonstrates the public nature of scientific enterprise, especially on issues that are politically relevant. When combined with greater ease of communication, from conventional media, such as newspapers, radio, and television, to more informal websites, what is normally a relatively private debate among scientists and experts can easily be shifted into the public arena. Overall, such exchanges contribute to a public impression that the science of global warming is 'contested', despite what many would argue is an overwhelmingly strong scientific case that global warming is occurring and human activity is a main driver of this change.

In the USA, perhaps more powerful than newspaper coverage have been other forms of media that rely on visual information, such as film, television, and the internet. Researchers have studied the effects of the 2004 Hollywood blockbuster film *The Day After Tomorrow*. With a huge viewing public (estimated at 21 million people in the USA alone), *The Day After Tomorrow* was a commercial success and also appears to have helped to promote climate change from an obscure scientific issue to one of popular public concern. In addition, the media coverage in glossy magazines, for example in *Time Magazine* in April 2006, and *Vanity Fair* in May 2006, has begun to convey a greater sense of urgency about climate change. Finally, widespread media coverage of emblematic impacts of climate change has also been stimulated by the international release of the documentary film *An Inconvenient Truth* by Al Gore, and by a growing number of television documentaries on climate change, such as *60 Minutes*, ABC News and HBO documentaries, in 2006. This rise in 'visual' media coverage suggests that in the last decade the 'availability heuristics' for promoting public understanding of climate change have risen dramatically.

The economists wade in

Economists have been involved with studying climate change from the very beginning of the IPCC process. There are two landmark publications that have had very different effects on the global warming debate. First, there was the publication of the controversial book *The Skeptical Environmentalist* by Bjørn Lomborg in English in 2001. In this and subsequent books, he argues that the cost of cutting global greenhouse emissions is extremely high and that those who suffer most from the effects of climate change are those in the poorest countries. He argues that a better use of this money would be poverty alleviation and rapid development of the Third World. As he suggests, if you are starving, you are not worried about the state of the planet for your children, you are worrying solely about having them at all.

This view, as you can imagine, was highly controversial. The second major landmark was the publication of the UK government-commissioned Stern Report on *The Economics of Climate Change* in 2006 (Cambridge University Press version first published in 2007). The report was led by Sir Nicholas Stern, then the adviser to the UK government on the economics of climate change and development reporting to the prime minister (then Tony Blair). The report states that if we do nothing, then the impacts of climate change could cost between 5% and 20% of world GDP every year. That means the whole world loses one-fifth of what it earns to address the impacts (discussed in Chapter 5). This of course puts climate change impacts on a completely different economic scale than was envisaged by Lomborg. This dire view of the future has been supported by a recent commentary by Martin Parry and colleagues in the journal *Nature* (June 2008). But the Stern Report does present some good news, because if we do everything we can to reduce global greenhouse gas emissions and ensure we adapt to the coming effects of climate change, this will cost us only 1% of world GDP every year. The Stern Report has been criticized on specifics by other economists – for example, does it use the right inherent discount rate? This is the rate economists use to take into account that consumption inherently has a lower value in the future than in the present. This is because future consumption should be discounted simply because it takes place in the future and people generally prefer the present to the future. For example William Nordhaus used inherent discount rates of up to 3 per cent, which means an environmental benefit occurring 25 years in the future is worth about half as much as the same benefit today. Stern argued that inherent discount rates were ethically inappropriate. The Stern Report has also been criticized for being overly optimistic about the costs of adapting to a low-carbon world. Roger Pielke Jr and colleagues in the journal *Nature* (April 2008) present a case that emissions scenarios used by the IPCC 2007 are too low and thus the technological and political challenge, and thus the cost, would be much higher. In June 2008 Sir Nicholas Stern did revise his estimated costs up to 2% of World GDP, not because of the above criticism, but because global warming was occurring faster than expected.

Nevertheless, the Stern Report sent seismic waves around the world. In the UK, most of my colleagues see the Stern Report and the winter of 2006/7 as the turning point when the public decided that climate change was real. It was as if people said to themselves, 'if the economists are worried about the cost of climate change, it must be real'.

Summary

So a combination of several factors – (1) the science of global warming essentially carried out by the mid-1960s, (2) the 'hockey stick' upturn in the global temperature data set which was first observed at the end of the 1980s, (3) our increased knowledge in the 1980s of how past climate has reacted to changes in atmospheric carbon dioxide, (4) our greater ability in the late 1970s and 1980s to model future changes in climate with supercomputers, (5) the emergence of global environmental awareness in the late 1980s, (6) the media's savage engagement in the confrontational nature of the debate and the huge interest in what some of my colleagues call 'climate porn', and (7) politicians and economists taking the threat of climate change seriously since the late 1990s – has led finally to recognition and acceptance of the global warming hypothesis.

Over the same period, thousands of scientists have turned their attention to understanding global warming. Landmarks have been the setting up of the Intergovernmental Panel on Climate Change (IPCC) in 1988 by the United Nations Environmental Panel and World Meteorological Organization; the publication of key reports by the IPCC in 1990, 1996, 2001, and 2007; the formal signature of the United Nations Framework Convention on Climate Change (UNFCCC) at the Rio Earth Summit in 1992; the subsequent Conference of the Parties (COP) at Kyoto in 1998, where the UNFCCC Protocols were formally accepted, the agreement of the 'Kyoto' Protocols in Bonn in July 2001, and the ratification of the Kyoto Protocol on the 16 February 2005.

Chapter 3
What is the evidence for climate change?

Past climate change

Climate change in the geological past has been reconstructed using a number of key archives, including marine and lake sediments, ice cores, cave deposits, and tree rings. These various records reveal that over the last 100 million years the Earth's climate has been cooling down, moving from the so-called 'greenhouse world' of the Cretaceous Period, when dinosaurs enjoyed warm and gentle conditions, through to the cooler and more dynamic 'ice house world' of today (see Figure 8). It may seem odd that in geological terms our planet is extremely cold, while this whole book is concerned with our great fears of global warming. This is because the very fact that there are huge ice sheets on both Antarctica and Greenland and nearly permanent sea ice in the Arctic Ocean makes the global climate very sensitive to changes in greenhouse gases.

This long-term, 100-million-year transition to colder global climate conditions was driven mainly by tectonic changes. These included the opening of the Tasmanian–Antarctic gateway and the Drake Passage, which isolated Antarctica from the rest of the world, the uplift of the Himalayas, and the closure of the Panama ocean gateway. There is also geological evidence that this cooling has been accompanied by a massive drop in the levels of

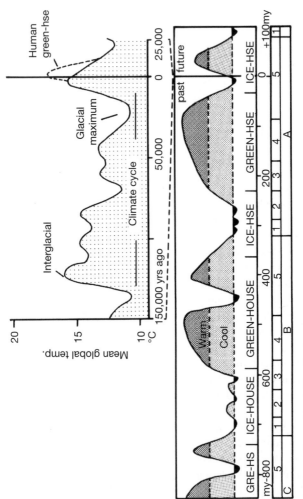

8. The anatomy of past climatic changes

atmospheric carbon dioxide. For example, 100 million years ago, during the time of the dinosaurs, atmospheric carbon dioxide levels could have been as much as five times higher than today.

These changes culminated in the glaciation of Antarctica about 35 million years ago and then the great northern hemisphere ice ages, which began 2.5 million years ago. Since the beginning of the great northern ice ages, the global climate has cycled from conditions that were similar or even slightly warmer than today, to full ice ages, which caused ice sheets over 3km thick to form over much of North America and Europe. Between 2.5 and 1 million years ago, these glacial–interglacial cycles occurred every 41,000 years, and since 1 million years ago they have occurred every 100,000 years. These great ice-age cycles are driven primarily by changes in the Earth's orbit with respect to the Sun. In fact, the world has spent over 80% of the last 2.5 million years in conditions colder than the present. Our present interglacial, the Holocene Period, started about 10,000 years ago and is an example of the rare warm conditions that occur between each ice age. The Holocene began with the rapid and dramatic end of the last ice age; in less than 4,000 years global temperatures increased by 6°C, relative sea level rose by 120m, atmospheric carbon dioxide increased by one-third, and atmospheric methane doubled.

It may seem strange in a book about global warming to suggest that we are currently in a geological 'ice house world'. This is, however, an important point when we look at the consequences of the world warming up, because, despite being in a relatively warm interglacial period, both poles are still glaciated, which is a rare occurrence in the geological history of our planet. Antarctica and Greenland are covered by ice sheets, and the majority of the Arctic Ocean is covered with sea ice. This means that there is a lot of ice that could melt in a warmer world, and, as we will see, this is one of the biggest unknowns that the future holds for our planet. The two glaciated poles also make the temperature gradient, or difference between the poles and the equator, extremely large, from an average of about +30°C at the equator down to −35°C or colder at the poles. This temperature gradient is one of the main reasons that we have a climate system, as excess heat from the tropics is exported both via the oceans and the atmosphere to the poles, which causes our weather. Geologically, we currently have one of the largest equator–pole temperature gradients, which leads to a very dynamic climate system. So our 'ice house' conditions cause our very energetic weather system, which is characterized by hurricanes, tornadoes, extra-tropical (temperate) winter storms, and monsoons. James Lovelock in his book *The Ages of Gaia* (new edition, 1995, p. 227) suggests that interglacials, like the Holocene Period, are the fevered state of our planet, which clearly over the last 2.5 million years prefers a colder average global temperature. Lovelock sees global warming as humanity just adding to the fever.

Climate, however, has not been constant during our interglacial, that is over the last 10,000 years. Palaeoclimate evidence suggests that the early Holocene was warmer than the 20th century. Throughout the Holocene, there have been millennial-scale climate events, called Dansgaard-Oeschger cycles, which involve a local cooling of 2°C. These events have had a significant influence on classical civilizations; for example, the cold arid event about 4,000 years ago coincides with the collapse of many classical civilizations, such as the Old Kingdom in Egypt.

The last of these millennial climate cycles was the Little Ice Age. This event is really two cold periods; the first follows the Medieval Warm Period, which ended 1,000 years ago, and is often correspondingly referred to as the Medieval Cold Period. The Medieval Cold Period played a role in extinguishing Norse colonies on Greenland and caused famine and mass migration in Europe. It started gradually before AD 1200 and ended at about AD 1650. The second cold period, more classically referred to as the Little Ice Age, may have been the most rapid and largest change in the North Atlantic region during the late Holocene, as suggested by ice-core and deep-sea sediment records. However, it is clear from records around the globe that the Little Ice Age and the Medieval Warm Period occurred only in northern Europe, north-east America, and Greenland (see Figure 9). Whenever the Little Ice Age is mentioned so too are the symbolic Ice Fairs that were held on the River Thames. However, the freezing of the River Thames had as much to do with the sluggish flow of the river until the port of London was built in the 1800s as the colder temperatures. There are four main data sets which have attempted to reconstruct temperatures for the northern hemisphere over the last millennium: tree rings, corals, ice cores, and/or the direct measurement of past temperatures from boreholes. First, it should be noted that the different data sets compare well with each other, which gives added confidence that we are seeing real temperature variations in these reconstructions. Second, the data show that the centuries before 1900 were much colder. They also show that the Medieval Warm Period and the Little Ice Age did occur, but that in much of the northern hemisphere little climate change can be

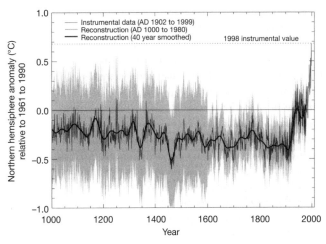

9. Northern hemisphere temperature reconstruction for the last 1,000 years

seen, with the exception of northern Europe. Without this last millennium data the instrumental temperature data set for the last 150 years would have no context. As it is, it can now be clearly shown that temperatures, at least for the northern hemisphere, have been warmer in the 20th century than at any other time during the last 1,000 years, revealing the so-called 'hockey stick'.

Recent climate change

The three main indicators of global warming are temperature, precipitation, and sea level. One of the key aims of scientists over the last couple of decades has been to estimate how these have changed since the industrial revolution and to see if there is any evidence for global warming being to blame. Below is the evidence for each of these parameters.

Temperature

As we have seen, temperatures for the northern hemisphere have been reconstructed for the last 1,000 years, providing a context to the 20th century. Temperatures for the last 150 years have been estimated from a number of sources, both direct thermometer-based indicators and proxy-based. What is a proxy? As used here and elsewhere, it is short for 'proxy variable'. The term 'proxy' is commonly used to describe a stand-in or substitute, as in 'proxy vote' or 'fighting by proxy'. In the same way, 'proxy variable' in the parlance of climatology means a measurable 'descriptor' that stands in for a desired (but unobservable) variable, such as past ocean or land temperature. So there is an assumption that you can use the proxy variable to estimate a climatic variable that you cannot measure directly. So, as we will see below, you can use the thickness of tree rings as a way of estimating past land temperatures; in this case, the tree-ring thickness is a proxy for temperature.

Thermometer-based indicators include sea-surface temperature (SST), marine air temperatures (MAT), land surface-air temperature, and temperatures in the free atmosphere, such as those measured by sensors on balloons. Borehole temperature measurements are defined as proxy-based because, despite the use of direct measurements of temperatures, these have been altered over time. Mathematical inversion procedures are required to translate the modern temperature in the boreholes into changes of ground temperature back through time. Other proxy-based methods include infrared satellite measurements and tree-ring width and thickness.

Thermometer-based measurements of air temperature have been recorded at a number of sites in North America and Europe as far back as 1760. The number of observation sites does not increase to sufficient worldwide geographical coverage to permit a global land average to be calculated until about the middle of the 19th century. SST and marine air temperatures were systematically recorded by ships from the mid-19th century, but even today the coverage of the southern hemisphere is extremely poor. All these data sets require various corrections to account for changing conditions and measurement techniques. For example, for land data each station has been examined to ensure that conditions have not varied through time as a result of changes in the measurement site, instruments used, instrument shelters, or the way monthly averages were computed, or the growth of cities around the sites, which leads to warmer temperatures caused by the urban heat island effect. In the IPCC 2007 science report, the influence of the urban heat island is acknowledged as real but negligible for the global temperature compilation (less than 0.006°C).

For SST and MAT, there are a number of corrections that have to be applied. First, up to 1941 most SST temperature measurements were made in sea water hoisted on deck in a bucket. Since 1941, most measurements have been made at the ships' engine water intakes. Second, between 1856 and 1910 there was a shift from wooden to canvas buckets, which changes the amount of cooling caused by evaporation that occurs as the water is being hoisted on deck. In addition, through this period there was a gradual shift from sailing ships to steamships, which altered the height of the ship decks and the speed of the ships, both of which can affect the evaporative cooling of the buckets. The other key correction that has to be made is for the global distribution of meteorological stations through time, which has varied greatly since 1870. But by making these corrections it is possible to produce a continuous record of global surface temperature for the last 100 years (1906 to 2005), which shows a global warming of 0.74°C ±0.05°C over this period.

What is so interesting about the 130-year temperature data set are the details, particularly as mentioned before the cooling observed in the 1960s and 1970s. One of the key tests for climate models, used to predict future climate changes, is whether they can reproduce the changes seen since 1870. These models are discussed in more detail in the next chapter but it should be noted that only by combining natural forcing (such as solar 11-year cycles and stratospheric aerosols from explosive volcanic eruptions), and anthropogenic forcing (greenhouse gases and sulphur aerosols) can the temperature record be simulated.

For the last 40 years, balloon data have been available. In 1958, an initial network of 540 stations was set up to release rawindsondes, or balloons, which were regularly released to measure temperature, relative humidity, and pressure through the atmosphere to a height of about 20km, where they burst. By the 1970s, the network had grown to 700–800 stations reporting twice daily. The balloon data set shows a general surface and lower troposphere warming over the last 30 years of about 0.1–0.2 °C per decade, which compares well with the instrumental record, which has a trend over the last 50 years of 0.13°C per decade.

Satellite-based proxy records have been available for the last 20 years and have been the source of some key controversies in the global warming debate. The advantage of satellite-mounted microwave sensors is that they have a global coverage, unlike the balloons which are predominately land-based and in the northern hemisphere. There are, however, some major problems with the microwave data set. First, the temperature record is based on eight different satellites, and despite overlapping measurement times, intercalibration between different instruments is problematic. Second, there is a spurious warming trend after 1990 of 0.03–0.04°C which is due to a drift in the orbital times, and a spurious cooling trend of 0.12°C per decade due to the reduced altitude or height of the satellites caused by friction with the atmosphere. Third, the height within the atmosphere at which the microwave sensor measures temperature is affected by the amount of ice crystals and raindrops in the atmosphere. Hence, if the planet is warming up, moisture will be found at great altitude, and the microwave sensor would in fact measure temperature much higher in the atmosphere, that is in the colder parts of the troposphere, thus giving a smaller temperature increase than that which actually occurred. It is unsurprising that reports on satellite recorded global temperature trends for the last 30 years have changed, as every new paper published contains yet another correction that must be considered. For example, huge controversy occurred when Christy and colleagues in 1995 deduced a global mean cooling trend of 0.05°C/decade for the period 1979–94, but obtained a warming trend of 0.09°C/decade over this period by removing the effects of El Niño and the climatic effect of the eruption of Mount Pinatubo. When the data set is corrected for decreasing satellite altitude, the global mean cooling turns into a warming of 0.07°C/decade. If the balloon, surface, and satellite data are compared, there is some agreement, and they show that the surface and lower troposphere have been warming up, while the stratosphere has been cooling down.

The IPCC collation of the published land-surface air and sea-surface temperatures from 1850 to 2005 includes all the corrections discussed above. These data are shown relative to the average temperature between 1961 and 1990 in Figure 10, and, as

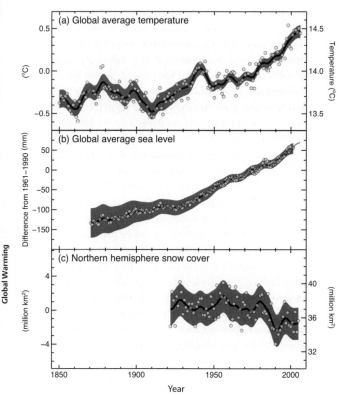

10. Temperature, sea level, and snow cover for the last 150 years

you can see, there has been a sharp warming from the start of the
1980s onwards. The mean global surface temperature has
increased by 0.74°C ±0.05°C over the last 100 years (1906 to
2005), and by 0.76°C since 1850 if the average between 1850 and
1899 and 2001 and 2005 is taken. Indirect indicators, such
as borehole temperatures and glacier shrinkage, provide
independent support for the observed warming. It is also noted
by the IPCC (2007) that the warming has not been globally

Global Warming

uniform. Warming in the Arctic has been double the global rate in recent decades.

Precipitation

There are two global precipitation data sets: 'Hulme' and the 'Global Historical Climate Network' (GHCN). Unfortunately, unlike temperature, rainfall and snow data are not as well documented and the records have not been carried out for as long. It is also known that precipitation over land tends to be underestimated by up to 10–15% owing to the effects of airflow around the collecting dish. Without correction of this effect, there is a spurious upward trend in global precipitation; after correction, there seems to be no statistically significant increase of global precipitation. However, there is clear evidence that since the 1980s atmospheric water content has increased over the land and ocean as well as in the upper troposphere. This is consistent with the extra water vapour that the warmer atmosphere can hold.

Though no discernible global trend in precipitation can be found at the moment, there is good evidence of significant regional changes. The IPCC reports that significant increases in precipitation have occurred in the eastern parts of North and South America, northern Europe, and northern and central Asia. It seems that seasonality of precipitation is also changing, for example in the high latitudes in the northern hemisphere, with increased rainfall in the winter and a decrease in the summer. Long-term drying trends have been observed on Sahel, in the Mediterranean, southern Africa, and parts of southern Asia. It has also been observed that the amount of rain falling during heavy 'extreme' rain events has increased, for example in the USA, Europe, the former Soviet Union, and China.

Relative global sea level

The IPCC has also put together a key data set of sea level. It shows that over the last 100 years, the global sea level has risen by about

12 to 22cm (Figure 10). Sea-level change is difficult to measure, as relative sea-level changes have been derived from two very different data sets – tide-gauges and satellites. In the conventional tide-gauge system, the sea level is measured relative to a land-based tide-gauge benchmark. The major problem is that the land surface is much more dynamic that one would expect, with a lot of vertical movements, and these become incorporated into the measurements. Vertical movements can occur as a result of normal geological compaction of delta sediments, the withdrawal of groundwater from coastal aquifers (both of which are discussed in more detail in Chapter 5, in the Coastline section), uplift associated with colliding tectonic plates (the most extreme of which is mountain-building such as in the Himalayas), or ongoing postglacial rebound and compensation elsewhere associated with the end of the last ice age. The latter is caused by the rapid removal of weight when the giant ice sheets melted, so that the land that has been weighed down slowly rebounds back to its original position. An example of this is Scotland, which is rising at a rate of 3mm per year, while England is still sinking at a rate of 2mm per year, despite the Scottish ice sheet having melted 10,000 years ago. In comparison, the simple problem with the satellite data is that it is too short, with the best data starting in January 1993, and this means it has to be combined with the tide-gauge data to look at long-term trends. However, the 1993 to 2007 data clearly show an increase of over 40mm in global sea level.

In summary, between 1961 and 2003 the global average sea level rose by 1.8mm per year, with the fastest rate being observed between 1993 and 2003 of 3.1mm per year. The 1993–2003 rate is made up of the following contributions: thermal expansion of the ocean contributed 1.6mm per year (~50%); Antarctic ice sheet 0.21mm (~7%); Greenland ice sheet 0.21mm (~7%); and glaciers and other ice caps 0.77mm per year (~25%); with approximately 0.3mm per year (10%) unaccounted for. These new data clearly show that the Greenland and Antarctic ice sheets have contributed to recent sea-level rise.

This is important because one of the biggest unknowns of global warming is how much the massive ice sheets over Greenland and Antarctica will melt. A key indicator of the expansion or contraction of these ice sheets is the sea ice that surrounds them. The state of the cryosphere (or the global ice) is extremely important, as shrinking of ice on land causes the sea level to rise. Unfortunately, submarines have already recorded a worrying thinning of the polar ice caps. Sea-ice draft is the thickness of the part of the ice that is submerged under the sea. In order to understand the effects of global warming on the cryosphere, it is important to measure how much ice is melting in the polar regions. Comparison of sea-ice draft data acquired on submarine cruises between 1993 and 1997 with similar data acquired between 1958 and 1976 indicates that the mean ice draft at the end of the melt season has decreased by about 1.3m in most of the deep-water portions of the Arctic Ocean, from 3.1m in 1958 to 1.8m in the 1990s. In summary, ice draft in the 1990s is over a metre thinner than four decades earlier. The main draft has decreased from over 3m to less than 2m, and the volume is down by some 40%. In addition, in 2000, for the first time in recorded history, a hole large enough to be seen from space opened in the sea ice above the North Pole. In 2007, satellites revealed the biggest retreat of arctic sea ice ever recorded. Moreover, measurements of the size of Greenland suggest that it is shrinking, by over 1,000 gigatonnes of ice since 2003, particularly at its coastal margins.

Other evidence for global warming

Other evidence for global warming comes from permafrost regions and weather patterns such as certain storm records. Permafrost exists in high-latitude and high-altitude areas, where it is so cold that the ground is frozen solid to a great depth. During the summer months, only the top metre or so of the permafrost becomes warm enough to melt, and this is called the 'active layer'. Already in Alaska there seems to have been a 3°C warming down to at least a metre over the last 50 years, showing that the active layer has become deeper. The maximum area cover by seasonal ground has decreased by 7% in the northern hemisphere since 1900, with a decrease in the spring of up to 15%. With the massive increases in atmospheric CO_2 predicted for the future, it is likely that there will be increases in the thickness of the active layer of the permafrost, or perhaps, in some areas, the complete disappearance of so-called discontinuous permafrost over the next century. This widespread loss of permafrost will produce a huge range of problems in local areas, as it will trigger erosion or subsidence, change hydrologic processes, and release into the atmosphere even more CO_2 and methane trapped as organic matter in the frozen layers. Hence changes in permafrost will reduce the stability of slopes and thus increase incidence of slides and avalanches. A more dynamic cryosphere will increase the natural hazards for people, structures, and communication links. Already, buildings, roads, pipelines, such as the oil pipelines in Alaska, and communication links are under threat.

There is evidence too that our weather patterns are changing. For example, in recent years massive storms and subsequent floods have hit China, Italy, England, Korea, Bangladesh, Venezuela, and Mozambique. In England in 2000, floods classified as 'once-in-30-years events' occurred twice in the same month. Moreover, in Britain the winter of 2000/1 was the wettest six months since records began in the 18th century, August 2008 was the wettest on record and British birds nest 12 ± 4 days earlier than 30 years previously. Insect species – including bees and termites – that need warm weather to survive are moving northward, and some have already reached England by crossing the Channel from France. While in the summer of 2003, 35,000 people died in an extreme heat wave in northern Europe, during which $100°F$ was recorded for the first time ever in Britain. In addition, glaciers in Europe are in retreat, particularly in the Alps and Iceland. Ice cover records from the Tornio River in Finland, which have been compiled since 1693, show that the spring thaw of the frozen river now occurs a month earlier.

There is also evidence that more storms are occurring in the northern hemisphere. Wave height in the North Atlantic Ocean has been monitored since the early 1950s, from lightships, Ocean Weather Stations, and more recently satellites. Between the 1950s and 1990s, the average wave height increased from 2.5m to 3.5m, an increase of 40%. Storm intensity is the major determinant of wave height, which provides evidence for an increase in storm activity over the last 40 years. This also fits with the observed increase in winter extra-tropical cyclones, that is those occurring in the mid-latitudes, which have increased markedly over the last 100 years, with significant rises in both the Pacific and Atlantic sectors since the early 1970s. There is also evidence for an increase in intense tropical hurricane activity since the 1970s in the North Atlantic.

What do the sceptics say?

One of the best ways to summarize the evidence for global warming and to persuade you, the reader, that there is evidence that humanity has already altered global climate, is to review what the sceptics say against the global warming hypothesis:

1) Ice-core data suggest atmospheric carbon dioxide responds to global temperature, therefore, atmospheric carbon dioxide cannot cause global temperature changes.

A detailed examination of the ice-core carbon dioxide data at the end of the last glacial period shows that the major stepwise increases occur at the same time as warming in Antarctica. It is known that during the last deglaciation, gradual warming in Antarctica occurred before steplike warming in the northern hemisphere. There is, therefore, excellent evidence that atmospheric carbon dioxide increases before overall global temperatures rise and the ice sheets begin to melt. In fact, there is clear evidence that Antarctic temperatures and atmospheric carbon dioxide levels are in step, demonstrating the central role of carbon dioxide as a climate amplifier. Moreover, time-series analysis of the last four glacial–interglacial cycles by the late Professor Sir Shackleton at the University of Cambridge suggests atmospheric carbon dioxide response up to 5,000 years before variations in global ice sheets. This has prompted many palaeoclimatologists to re-evaluate the role of atmospheric carbon dioxide, placing it now as a primary driving force of past climate instead of a secondary response and feedback.

2) Every data set showing global warming has been corrected or tweaked to achieve this desired result.

For people who are not regularly involved in science, this seems to be the biggest problem with the whole 'global warming has happened' argument. As I have shown, all the data sets covering the last 150 years require some sort of adjustment. This, though, is part of the scientific process. For example, if great care had not been taken over the spurious trends in the global precipitation database we would now assume that global precipitation was increasing. Moreover, as science moves forward incrementally, it gains more and more understanding and insight into the data sets it is constructing. This constant questioning of all data and interpretations is the core strength of science: each new correction or adjustment is due to a greater understanding of the data and the climate system and thus each new study adds to the confidence that we have in the results. This is why the IPCC report refers to the 'weight of the evidence', since our confidence in science increases if similar results are obtained from very different sources.

3) Solar output and sunspot activity control the past temperatures.

This is something both the sceptics and non-sceptics agree upon. Of course, sunspots and also volcanic activity have influenced past temperatures. For example, the cooling of the 1960s and 1970s is clearly linked to changes in the sunspot cycle. The difference between the two camps is that the sceptics put more weight on the importance of these natural variations. Though great care has been taken to understand how the minor variations in solar output affect global climate, this is still one of the areas which contain many unknowns and uncertainties. However, climate models combining our current state-of-the-art knowledge concerning all radiative forcing, including greenhouse gases (see Table 1) and sunspots, are able to simulate the global temperature curve for the last 130 years. Figure 11 shows the separate natural and anthropogenic forcing on global climate for the last 130 years and the combination of the two. This provides confidence in both models and also an understanding of the relative influence of natural versus anthropogenic forcing.

4) Satellite data cast doubt on the models.

Again, before the satellite data were clearly understood, they did suggest that over the last 25 years there had been a slight cooling. The iterative process of science – the re-examination of data and assumptions concerning the data – clearly showed that there were some major inconsistencies within the satellite data: first, as a result of trying to compare the data from different instruments on different satellites; and, second, because of the need to adjust the altitude of the satellite as its orbit shrinks as a result of friction with the atmosphere. The final problem with the satellite data is that 20 years is just too short a time period to find a temperature trend with any confidence. This is because climatic cycles or events will have a major influence on the record and will not be averaged out: for example, the sunspot cycle is 11 years, El Niño–Southern Oscillation is 3–7 years, and the North Atlantic Oscillation is 10 years. So which of these cycles is picked up by the 20-year satellite data will strongly influence the direction of the temperature trend.

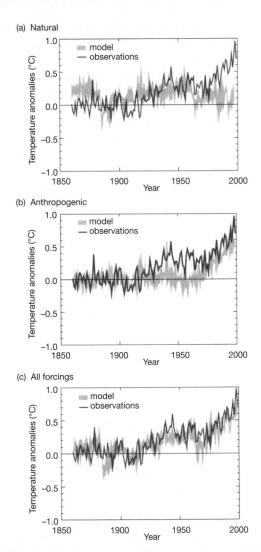

(a) Natural

(b) Anthropogenic

(c) All forcings

11. Simulated annual global mean surface temperatures compared to observed temperatures

Summary

Over the last 150 years, significant changes in climate have been recorded; including a 0.74°C increase in average global temperatures over the last 100 years, sea-level rise of over 40mm, significant shifts in the seasonality and intensities of precipitation, changing weather patterns, significant retreat of Arctic sea ice and nearly all continental glaciers. We know that in the last 150 years, the 12 warmest years on record have all occurred within the last 13 years, with 1998 the warmest year, followed by 2005, 2002, 2003, and 2004, while 2007 was the eighth warmest year on record. The IPCC 2007 report states that the evidence for global warming is unequivocal and there is very high confidence that this warming is due to human activity.

What is the evidence for climate change?

Chapter 4
How do you model the future?

You may not believe this, but the whole of human society operates on knowing the future, particularly the weather. For example, a farmer in India knows when the monsoon rains will come next year and so when to plant his crops, while a farmer in Indonesia knows there are two monsoon rains next year so he can plant crops twice. This is based on their knowledge of the past, as the monsoons have always come at about the same time each year in living memory. But such a prediction goes deeper than this as it influences every part of our lives. Our houses are built for the local climate – in Britain that means central heating but no air-conditioning, while in the southern USA it is vice versa. Roads, railways, airports, offices, cars, trains, and so on are all designed for the local climate. This is why in the spring of 2003 a centimetre of snow one afternoon effectively shut down London, while Toronto can easily deal with and function with half a metre of snow. In Europe in 2003, 35,000 people died in the summer heat wave in temperatures that regularly occur in the tropics, while Australians go into shock if the temperature drops below 50°F. The problem with global warming is that it changes the rules. The past weather of an area cannot be relied upon to tell you what the future will hold. So we have to develop new ways of predicting the future, so that we can plan our lives and so that human society can continue to fully function. So we have to model the future.

There is a whole hierarchy of climate models, from relatively simple box models to the extremely complex three-dimensional general circulation models (GCMs). Each has a role in examining and furthering our understanding of the global climate system. However, it is the complex three-dimensional general circulation models which are used to predict future global climate. These comprehensive climate models are based on physical laws represented by mathematical equations that are solved using a three-dimensional grid over the globe. To obtain the most realistic simulations, all the major parts of the climate system must be represented in sub-models, including atmosphere, ocean, land surface (topography), cryosphere, and biosphere, as well as the processes that go on within them and between them. Most global climate models have at least some representation of each of these components. Models that couple together both the ocean and atmosphere components are called Atmosphere–Ocean General Circulation Models (AOGCMs). The development of climate models over the last two decades is shown in Figure 12. Models of different parts of the climate system are first developed separately and then coupled into the comprehensive climate models. For example, the Met Office Hadley Centre model is the first AOGCM which now has a fully coupled 'dynamic vegetation' model. This is important because it has long been known that vegetation has an influence on climate; thus climate changes can affect the vegetation and those changes in vegetation can have an effect on climate. For example, the Amazon rainforest recycles about half the precipitation that falls, maintaining a moist continental interior which would otherwise be dry.

One of the key aspects of climate models is the detail in which they can reconstruct the world; this is usually termed 'spatial resolution'. In general, the current generation of AOGCMs have a resolution or detail of the atmosphere of one point every 250km by 250km in the horizontal and about 1km in the vertical above the boundary layer. This would mean the atmosphere above the

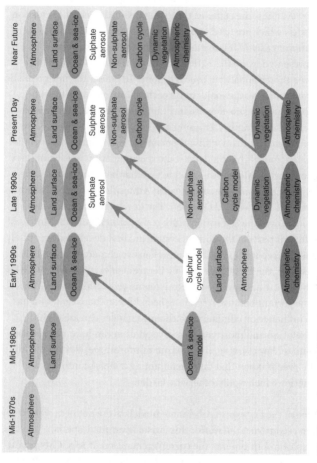

Global Warming

Mid-1970s	Mid-1980s	Early 1990s	Late 1990s	Present Day	Near Future
Atmosphere	Atmosphere	Atmosphere	Atmosphere	Atmosphere	Atmosphere
	Land surface	Land surface	Land surface	Land surface	Land surface
		Ocean & sea-ice	Ocean & sea-ice	Ocean & sea-ice	Ocean & sea-ice
		Sulphur cycle model	Sulphate aerosol	Sulphate aerosol	Sulphate aerosol
			Non-sulphate aerosols	Non-sulphate aerosol	Non-sulphate aerosol
			Carbon cycle model	Carbon cycle	Carbon cycle
		Land surface	Dynamic vegetation	Dynamic vegetation	Dynamic vegetation
		Atmosphere	Atmospheric chemistry	Atmospheric chemistry	Atmospheric chemistry
		Ocean & sea-ice model			
		Atmospheric chemistry			

12. **The development of climate models, past, present, and future**

British Isles would be represented by only 10 points. The resolution of a typical ocean model is about 200–400m in the vertical and 125–250km in the horizontal. Equations are typically solved for every simulated 'half hour' of a model run. Many physical processes, such as cloud and ocean convection, of course take place on a much smaller scale than the model can resolve. Therefore, the effects of small-scale processes have to be lumped together, and this is referred to as 'parametrization'. Many of these parametrizations are, however, checked with separate 'small-scale-process models' to validate the scaling up of these smaller influences. The reason that the spatial scale is limited is that comprehensive AOGCMs are very complex and use a huge amount of computer time to run. At the moment, much of the improvement in computer processing power that has occurred over the last decade has been used to improve the representation of the global climate system by coupling more models directly to the AOGCMs. It is important to run these models numerous times because, as discussed below, there are many parts of the climate system for which the future parameters are uncertain. For example, the future human greenhouse gas emissions, which are not fixed, as they will depend on many variables, such as the global economy, development of technology, political agreements, and personal lifestyles. Hence, you could produce the most complete model in the world taking two years to simulate the next 100 years, but you would have only one prediction of the future based on only one estimate of future emissions which might be completely wrong. Individual models are therefore run many times with different inputs to provide a range of changes in the future. In fact, the IPCC have consulted the results of multiple runs of 23 different AOGCMs to provide the basis for their predictions. Of course, as computer processing power continues to increase, both this representation of coupled climate systems and the spatial scale will continue to improve.

So what are the unknowns and why do we need to run many different model scenarios? Is there not just one view of the future?

Unfortunately not, and below each of the unknowns is described in more detail, along with how they affect our model predictions for the future.

Carbon cycle

One of the fundamental considerations for the AOGCMs is not whether carbon dioxide influences global temperatures, but rather the extent to which it influences global temperatures. This is not only because of the direct effect of the carbon dioxide but also because of the many secondary influences and other climate feedbacks, such as aerosols, ocean circulation, and so on, which may even cool the climate system. The first problem is estimating how much of the anthropogenic carbon dioxide makes it into the atmosphere. You will be surprised to know that about half of all our carbon emissions are absorbed by the natural carbon cycle and do not end up in the atmosphere, but rather in the oceans and the terrestrial biosphere. This leads us to realize that we need to understand the present-day carbon cycle in order to understand the amount of carbon dioxide that will end up in the atmosphere.

The Earth's carbon cycle is extremely complicated, with both sources and sinks of carbon dioxide. Figure 13 shows the global carbon reservoirs in GtC (gigatonnes, or 1,000 million tonnes) and fluxes (the ins and outs of carbon in GtC per year). These indicated figures are annual averages over the period 1980–9. It must be remembered that the component cycles have been simplified, and the figures only present average values. The amount of carbon stored and transported by rivers, particularly the anthropogenic portion, is currently very poorly quantified and is not shown here. Evidence is accumulating that many of the fluxes can vary significantly from year to year. In contrast to the static view conveyed in figures like this one, the carbon system is dynamic, and coupled to the climate system on seasonal, inter-annual, and

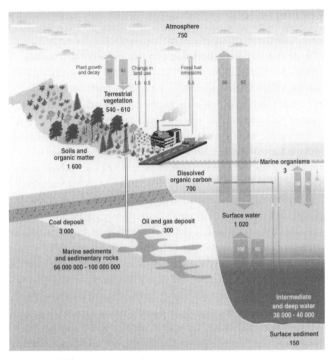

13. A simplified version of the present carbon cycle

decadal timescales. The most interesting figure is that the surface ocean takes up just less than half the carbon dioxide produced by industry per year. However, this is one of the most poorly known figures and there is still considerable debate over whether the oceans will continue to be such a large sink or absorber of our pollution. As we will see in Chapter 6, one of the great surprises recently has been the unexpected experimental results which suggest that the Amazon rainforest could be absorbing large quantities of atmospheric carbon dioxide. The key question we need to ask, if indeed this is the case, is: for how long will the oceans and the Amazon rainforest continue to absorb carbon dioxide?

Cooling effects

As well as the warming effects of the greenhouse gases, the Earth's climate system is complicated in that that there are also cooling effects (see Figure 14 for the IPCC summary of both warming and cooling effects). This includes the amount of particles in the air (which are technically called aerosols, many of which come from human pollution such as sulphur emissions from power stations) and these have a direct effect on the amount of solar radiation that hits the Earth's surface. Aerosols may have significant local or regional impact on temperature. In fact, the AOGCMs have now factored them into the computer simulations of global warming, and they provide an explanation of why industrial areas of the planet have not warmed as much as previously predicted. Water vapour is a greenhouse gas, but, at the same time, the upper white surface of clouds reflects solar radiation back into space. This reflection is called 'albedo' – and clouds and ice have a high albedo and so reflect large quantities of solar radiation from surfaces on Earth. Predicting what will happen to the amount and types of clouds, and the extent of global ice in the future, creates huge difficulties in calculating the exact effect of global warming. For example, if the polar ice cap melts, the albedo will be significantly reduced, as this ice would be replaced by vegetation or open water, both of which absorb heat rather than reflecting it like white snow or ice. This would produce a positive feedback, enhancing the effects of global warming.

Emission models of the future

A critical problem with trying to predict future climate is predicting the amount of carbon dioxide emissions that will be produced in the future. This will be influenced by population growth, economic growth, Third World development, fossil-fuel usage, the rate at which we switch to alternative energy, the rate of deforestation, and the effectiveness of international agreements to cut emissions. Out of all the systems that we are trying to model

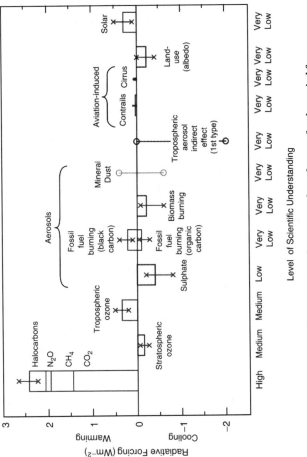

14. Global, annual-mean radiative forcings due to a number of agents for the period from pre-industrial to present

into the future, humanity is by far the most complicated and unpredictable. If you want to understand the problem of predicting what will happen in the next 100 years, imagine yourself in 1909 and what you would have predicted the world to be like in 2009. In 1909, the British Empire was the dominant world power due to the industrial revolution and the use of coal. Would you have predicted the switch to a global economy based on oil after the Second World War, or the explosion of car use, or the general availability of air travel? Even 15 years ago, it would have been difficult to predict the budget airlines which allow for such cheap flights throughout Europe and the USA.

So what the IPCC has done is to produce six scenarios of what the future could be like depending on the factors above. These are based on the IPCC Special Report on Emission Scenarios (SRES) of 2000. The SRES in terms of carbon dioxide equivalent in the atmosphere in 2100 are B1 (600ppm), A1T (700ppm), B2 (800ppm), A1B (850ppm), A2 (1,250), and A1Fl (1,500ppm) – remember we are currently at about 380ppm. The IPCC also has a seventh scenario for illustrative purposes, which is at the 'Constant Year 2000' concentrations, as this shows the climate change we have already instigated. However, these emissions scenarios have been heavily criticized. The biggest criticism is that the emissions scenarios are too generous, because, as many experts point out, we are already putting more carbon dioxide into the atmosphere per year than the most dire IPCC predictions. In the 1990s, carbon dioxide emissions increased by 1.1% per year; between 2000 and 2004 they had increased to more than 3%.

Future global temperatures and sea level

Twenty-three AOGCMs have been run using selected future carbon dioxide emission scenarios for the IPCC 2007 report, to produce global average temperature changes that may occur by 2100. This is a significant change from the IPCC 2001 report, in which only seven of these models were used. These climate models using the full likely range show that the global mean surface temperature could rise by between 1.1°C and 6.4°C by 2100 (see Figure 15). Using the best estimates for the six emission scenarios, then this range is 1.8°C to 4°C by 2100. Model experiments show that even if all radiation forcing agents were held at a year 2000 constant, there would still be an increase of 0.1°C per decade over the next 20 years. This is mainly due to the slow response of the ocean. Interestingly, the choice of emission scenario has little effect on the temperature rise to 2030, making this a very robust estimate. All models thus suggest twice the rate of temperature increase in the next two decades compared with the 20th century. What is significant is that the choices we make now in terms of global emissions will have a significant effect on global warming after 2030.

Again, using the 23 different carbon dioxide emission scenarios, the IPCC has projected global mean sea level up to 2100. The AOGCMs predict an increase in global mean sea level of between 18cm and 59cm. These estimates are lower than those in the IPCC 2001 report, the reason being because they have taken out the possible contribution of ice flow. Although ice flow rates increased between 1992 and 2003 in both Greenland and Antarctica, it is unknown whether this contribution will continue. If the contribution is linear with surface warming, then another 10cm to 20cm can be added to the sea-level estimates, giving a range of 28cm to 79cm by 2100. One of the biggest unknowns in global warming is what will happen to Greenland and Antarctica in the next 100 years, as there is a lot of evidence that they are starting to melt (see Chapter 6). There is also scientific debate about what may happen to both the Greenland and Antarctic ice sheets beyond the next 100 years. Some scientists believe what happens in the next 100 years will determine the future of these ice sheets. One prediction suggests that though the Greenland ice sheet will not collapse in the next 100 years, global warming will start a

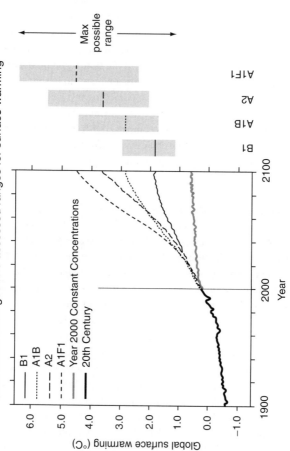

15. **Global temperatures of the 21st century.**

process that will be irreversible and Greenland will be free of ice within the next 1,000 years.

What the sceptics say

One of the best ways to summarize the problems of modelling the global warming future is to review what the sceptics say, as they have many valid points and provide a basis from which our models should be improved.

1) Clouds can have both a positive and negative feedback on global climate; how do we know they will not reduce the effects of global warming so that it occurs to a negligible degree?

As has been the case since the very first IPCC report in 1990, the greatest uncertainty in future predictions is the role of the clouds and their interaction with radiation. Clouds can both absorb and reflect radiation, thereby cooling the surface, and absorb and emit long-wave radiation, thus warming the surface. The competition between these effects depends on a number of factors: height, thickness, and radiative properties of clouds. The radiative properties and formation and development of clouds depend on the distribution of atmospheric water vapour, water drops, ice particles, atmospheric aerosols, and cloud thickness. The physical basis of how clouds are represented or parametrized in the AOGCMs has greatly improved through the inclusion of bulk representations of cloud microphysical properties in the cloud water budget equations. However, clouds still represent a significant source of potential error in climate simulations. It is still controversial whether clouds help warm or cool the planet and both situations are found in the various AOGCMs. However, it is interesting that even in those AOGCMs in which clouds cause a cooling effect, this effect is not strong enough to counter the other warming trends.

2) Different models give different results, so how can we trust any of them?

This is a frequent response from many people not familiar with modelling, as there is a feeling that somehow science must be able to predict an exact future. However, in no other walk of life do we expect this precision. For example, you would never expect to get a perfect prediction of which horse will win a race or which football team will emerge triumphant. The truth is that none of the climate models is exactly right. But what they provide is the best estimate that we have of the future. Now this view of the future is strengthened by the use of more than one model, because each model has been developed by different groups of scientists around the world, using different assumptions and different computers, and thus they provide their own particular future prediction. What causes scientists to have confidence in the model results is that they all roughly predict the same trend in global temperature and sea level for the next 100 years. One of the great strengths of the 2007 IPCC report is that it used 23 international models, compared to 7 in 2001, to produce future predictions. Another strength of this large-scale multiple model approach is that scientists can also give an estimation of how confident they are in the model results and also a range of possible predictions. The day that scientists give an exact estimate of what is going to happen and when is the day they will lose all credibility, rather like being told to invest in the US stock market just before the 1929 crash as stock markets can never go down, or being sold a mortgage in the early 1980s in the UK and being told that there is no way the housing market will crash.

3)   Climate models fail to predict abrupt weather conditions.

AOGCMs are not able to predict abrupt weather events because their spatial resolution is too coarse; for example, the whole of the British Isles is represented by 10 points. This has led to the accusation by the sceptics that the random or chaotic factors which influence our day-to-day weather must also influence our climate. It has been known since the late 1960s that weather patterns are chaotic, as the Earth's climate system is sensitive to extremely small perturbations in initial conditions. For example, extremely slight changes in air pressure over the USA have an influence on the direction and duration of a hurricane. We all know that this sensitivity limits the prediction accuracy of detailed weather forecasts to about two weeks; sometimes it feels like two days. However, predictability of climate is not limited in the same way as the prediction of the weather because the longer-term systematic influences on the atmosphere are not reliant on the initial conditions. So the longer-term trends in regional and global climate are not controlled by small-scale influences. However, what the global warming sceptics are correct about is that at present we cannot model abrupt climate changes, that may occur in the future. These potential surprises are discussed in Chapter 6.

4) Climate models fail to reconstruct or predict natural variability.

The global climate system contains cyclic variations which occur on a decade or sub-decade timescale. The most famous is El Niño, which is a change in both ocean and atmospheric circulation in the Pacific region occurring every three to seven years that has a major influence on the rest of the global climate. Sceptics argue that climate models have been unable to simulate satisfactorily these events in the past. However, climate models have become better at reconstructing these past variations in El Niño–Southern Oscillation (ENSO), North Atlantic Oscillation (NAO), and related Arctic Oscillation (AO) as there has been an increasing realization that these have a profound impact upon regional climate (see Chapter 5, El Niño–Southern Oscillation section, for further details). Most models are able to depict these natural variations, picking out particularly the 1976 climate shift which occurred in the Pacific Ocean. All the AOGCMs have predicted outcomes for ENSO and NAO for the next 100 years. However, a lot of improvement is required before there will be confidence in the model predictions. It is, though, testament to the realism of the AOGCMs that they can indeed reconstruct and predict future trends in these short-term oscillations.

5) The thermohaline circulation is not properly characterized in the climate models.

The deep, or thermohaline, circulation (THC) of the world's oceans is one of the basic building blocks of the coupled Atmosphere–Ocean GCMs, hence the simulations of the thermohaline circulation for the present day and the past are very good. However, uncertainties concerning the modelling of the future of the THC come from the complexities controlling deep-water formation, including the interplay in the large-scale atmospheric forcing between the warming and evaporation in the low latitudes and cooling and increased precipitation at high latitudes. In addition, ENSO can play a part by altering the freshwater balance of the tropical Atlantic. Add to this the uncertainties in the representation both of the small-scale flows over sills and through narrow straits and of ocean convection, which further limit the ability of the models to simulate situations involving substantial change in the THC. Hence most future predictions from AOGCMs have a similar or slightly reduced THC to the present. One way modellers get round the problem of having a slightly simplified representation of the ocean circulation in the AOGCMs is to run very high-resolution ocean models off-line. So you can run hundreds of different forcings on the oceans over hundreds of simulated years very quickly, and this is where our understanding of the sensitivity of the ocean comes from.

6) AOGCMs fail to reconstruct past climate, particularly the last ice age.

Past climates are an important test for global climate models. The biggest climate shift, for which we have many palaeoclimate reconstructions, is that of the last ice age, which ended about 10,000 years ago. A comparison between palaeoclimate data for the most extreme stage of the ice age, which occurred 18,000 years ago, suggests that the global climate models are rather good (see p. 451 of the IPCC Science Report 2007). It shows that the AOGCMs used for predicting future climate can do a good job of reconstructing the extreme conditions of an ice age – sea level 120m lower, 6°C drop in global temperatures, atmospheric carbon dioxide one-third lower, and atmospheric methane halved. One important observation is that the models are conservative, and they systematically underestimated the climatic changes. This means we can assume that the future climate predictions are also conservative, and thus climate change is very likely to be at the top end of the estimates.

7) Galactic cosmic rays (GCRs) are ignored in the current climate models, which invalidates the models.

Galactic cosmic rays are high-energy particles that cause ionization in the atmosphere and may, therefore, affect cloud formation. GCRs vary inversely with solar variability because of the effect of solar wind. This is an excellent example of how climate science progresses by discovering new knowledge and, if it is important enough, adding it into the climate models. Very little is known about this newly discovered external forcing, GCRs, so research is continuing into this phenomenon to see if it has a sufficiently large effect to be included in the climate models. Unfortunately, it affects one of the least well-understood processes in our climate system – that of cloud formation. But the discovery that GCRs may influence climate does not invalidate the climate models, because it is all part of the progressive nature of science. We do not know everything about the climate system and we never will. Our understanding will continually improve as science progresses; hence, model predictions of the future are continually improving. It should, however, be remembered that these models are based on the present understanding of the climate system and will inevitably change in the future.

Summary

Using a wide range of possible carbon emissions over the next 100 years, the climate models suggest the global mean surface temperature could rise by between 1.1°C and 6.4°C by 2100. Using the best estimates for the six emission scenarios, then this range is 1.8°C to 4°C by 2100. However, we must remember that global carbon dioxide emissions are already rising faster than the most dire of the IPCC emission scenarios. The models also predict an increase in global mean sea level of between 18cm and 59cm. If the contribution from the melting of Greenland and Antarctica is included, then this increases the range to between 28cm and 79cm by 2100. This is assuming a continued linear response between global temperatures and ice sheets, which is unlikely, and thus sea-level rise could be much higher. However, some leading climate scientists have voiced their concern that the IPCC 2007 predictions are too conservative. For example, Professor Jim Hansen of Columbia University suggests that if we reach 450ppm carbon dioxide then we may have passed the tipping point for the irreversible melting of Greenland and the West Antarctic ice sheet. If this happens, then we may see even larger rises in sea level in this century. Hence Hansen suggests that, if we are to save the ice sheets, we need to return to a global level of 350ppm as quickly as possible.

Chapter 5
What are the possible future impacts?

As discussed in previous chapters, there is strong evidence to suggest that humanity's greenhouse gas emissions have already started to influence our climate. The most sophisticated and powerful computer models suggest global warming will cause major climatic changes by the end of the 21st century. These changes will potentially have wide-ranging effects on the natural environment as well as on human societies and our economies. Estimates have been made concerning the potential direct impacts on various socioeconomic sectors, but in reality the full consequences are complicated to predict because impacts on one sector have an indirect effect on others. We are only just realizing how climate change policies can have negative effects on society. For example, as discussed later in this chapter, the recent rush to produce biofuels to mitigate global warming may have contributed to food price rises because of competition for land.

To assess these potential impacts, it is necessary to estimate the extent and magnitude of climate change, especially at national and local levels. For example, the IPCC 2007 reports look at the impacts on a continental level. There are also a number of excellent national reports and tools, such as the US National Assessment Synthesis Team 2001 and the UK Climate Impacts Programme (UKCIP) 2008. The UKCIP website with its interactive tools is a model for other countries as it allows anyone to assess the impacts of climate change in the UK. This is becoming an essential tool for policymakers and businesses alike in the UK.

What is dangerous climate change?

One of the most important questions for scientists and policymakers is what is dangerous climate change? Of course, this does depend on where you live. For example, if you are one of the small island nations, any sea-level rise could be considered dangerous because it directly results in loss of land. However, on the bigger picture, if we are to cut global greenhouse emissions we need a realistic target concerning the degree of global temperature increase with which we can cope. In February 2005, the British government convened an international science meeting at Exeter, UK, to discuss this very topic. This was a very political science meeting, as the UK government was looking for a recommendation to take to the G8 meeting in Gleneagles. In 2005, Britain was both the chair of the G8 and president of the EU, and the then prime minister Tony Blair wished to push forward internationally his joint agenda of climate change and poverty alleviation in Africa. The meeting did come up with a 'magic number' of 2°C above pre-industrial average temperature: below this threshold, there seem to be both winners and losers due to regional climate change, but above this figure everyone seems to lose. Table 2 summarizes some of the big climate changes that could occur and at what temperature increase. It isn't just this particular meeting that has come up with the magic 2°C limit; many other researchers, including at the IPCC, have arrived at similar conclusions from very different backgrounds and starting assumptions. Figure 16 shows the numbers of people estimated to be at risk from water shortages, hunger, malaria, and flooding by 2080.

Again, 2°C seems to be at the point where the numbers increase radically, so 2°C has become a powerful and important symbol of the challenges facing human society. The major problem is that it

Table 2. Impacts of global warming with increasing global average temperatures

How much is too much?	
1–2°C Above pre-industrial	• Major impacts on ecosystems and species. • Increase of heatwaves, droughts, floods and spread of infectious disease.
2–3°C	• Major loss of coral reef ecosystem and other species. • Large impacts on agriculture, water resources and health. • Significant increase in droughts and extreme rainfalls. • Up to 74cm sea level rise in next 100 years. • Terrestrial carbon sink becomes a source, accelerating global warming.
1–3°C ?	• Greenland ice-cap starts to melt (7m).
1–4°C ?	• North Atlantic circulation collapses.
3–4°C	• Major species extinction.
2–4.5°C ?	• West Antarctic ice sheet collapses (5m).
4–5°C	• 1–3 billion people suffer from water scarcity. • Food yields fall everywhere, global production plummets. • Fifth of world population effected by flooding. • Significant increase in human deaths due to malnutrition, disease, heatwave, flood and drought.
5–6°C or higher	• Don't go there.

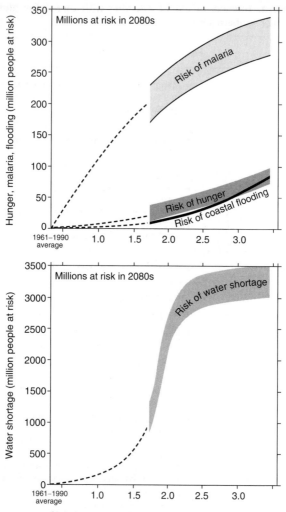

16. **Climate change risks as a function of increasing global temperatures**

is unlikely we can keep global temperature increases down to 2°C, as we have already seen temperature increase by 0.76°C, and even if we kept atmospheric carbon dioxide levels at the 2000 levels that would still add at least another 0.6°C. So without doing anything, we are already up to nearly 1.4°C. Below, we look at the general effects of global warming to give you an idea of what the future may hold.

Extreme events and society's coping range

The single biggest problem with global warming is our inability to predict the future. Humanity can live, survive, and even flourish in extreme climates from the Arctic to the Sahara, but problems arise when the predictable extremes of local climate are exceeded. For example, heat waves, storms, droughts, and floods in one region may be considered fairly normal weather in another. This is because each society has a coping range, a range of weather with which it can deal. Figure 17 shows the theoretical effect of combining the coping range with climate change. In our present climate, the coping range encompasses nearly all the variation in weather with maybe only one or two extreme events. As the climate moves gently to its new average, if the coping range stays the same then many more extreme events occur. For example, in the historically mild climate of Britain, homes are built with central heating but not air-conditioning. As summer temperatures increase and heat waves like 2003 become common, then the coping range of our homes will be exceeded and we will need air-conditioning.

One of the biggest challenges of global warming is to start to build as much flexibility and resilience into societies' coping ranges as possible. To do this, we must take the latest predictions of the IPCC and apply these across the globe to help protect people and their environments. As we have seen, the IPCC 2007 report estimates that global mean surface temperature could rise by between 1.1 and 6.4°C by 2100, there will be significant regional

Global Warming

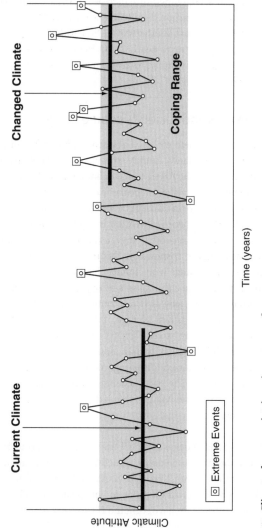

17. Climate change, society's coping range, and extreme events

changes in precipitation, and global mean sea level could rise by between at least 18cm and 59cm by 2100. Future climate change will have impacts on all factors affecting human society, including coastal regions, storms and floods, heat waves and droughts, health, water resources, agriculture, and biodiversity. Below, each of these key areas of concern and the possible impacts of climate change are reviewed. What cannot be assessed are the impacts if climate change occurs more abruptly, and this possibility is discussed in Chapter 6.

Coastline

As we have seen, the IPCC reports that sea level could rise by between 18cm and 59cm in the next 100 years, primarily through the thermal expansion of the oceans. If we include a simplistic assumption about Greenland and Antarctica, this could rise to 28cm to 79cm by 2100. This prediction is of major concern to all coastal areas, as rising sea levels will reduce the effectiveness of coastal defences against storms and floods, and increase the instability of cliffs and beaches. In Britain, the USA, and the rest of the developed world, the response to this danger has been to add another few feet to the height of sea walls around property on the coast, the abandoning of some poorer-quality agricultural land to the sea (as it is no longer worth the expense of protecting it), and the enhancement of legal protection for coastal wetlands, being nature's best defence against the sea. However, globally, there are some nations based on small islands and river deltas that face a much more urgent situation.

For small island nations, such as the Maldives in the Indian Ocean and the Marshall Islands in the Pacific, a 1m rise in sea level would flood up to 75% of the dry land, making the islands uninhabitable. Interestingly, it is also these countries, which rely on tourism, that have some of the highest fossil-fuel emissions per head of population. However, there is a different twist to the story if we consider nations where a significant portion of the population live by river deltas; these include, for example, Bangladesh, Egypt, Nigeria, and Thailand. A World Bank report in 1994 concluded that human activities on the deltas, such as fresh-water extraction, were causing these areas to sink much faster than any predicted rise in sea level, increasing their vulnerability to storms and floods.

In the case of Bangladesh, over three-quarters of the country is within the deltaic region formed by the confluence of the Ganges, Brahmaputra, and Meghna rivers. Over half the country lies less than 5m above sea level; thus flooding is a common occurrence. During the summer monsoon a quarter of the country is flooded. Yet these floods, like those of the Nile, bring with them life as well as destruction. The water irrigates and the silt fertilizes the land. The fertile Bengal delta supports one of the world's most dense populations, over 110 million people in 140,000 square kilometres. But the monsoon floods have been getting worse throughout the 1990s. Every year, the Bengal delta should receive over 1 billion tonnes of sediment and a 1,000 cubic kilometres of fresh water. This sediment load balances the erosion of the delta both by natural processes and human activity. However, the Ganges River has been diverted in India into the Hooghly Channel for irrigation. The reduced sediment input is causing the delta to subside. Exacerbating this is the rapid extraction of fresh water.

In the 1980s, 100,000 tube wells and 20,000 deep wells were sunk, increasing the fresh-water extraction sixfold. Both these projects are essential to improving the quality of life for people in this region, but have produced a subsidence rate of up to 2.5cm per year, one of the highest rates in the world. Using estimates of subsidence rate and global warming sea-level rise, the World Bank has estimated that by the end of the 21st century, the relative sea level in Bangladesh could rise by as much as 1.8m. In a worst-case scenario, they estimated that this would result in a loss of up to 16% of land, supporting 13% of the population, and producing 12% of the current gross domestic product (GDP). Unfortunately, this scenario does not take any account of the devastation of the mangrove forest and the associated fisheries. Moreover, increased landward intrusions of salt water would further damage water quality and agriculture.

Another example of a threatened coastline is the Nile delta, which is one of the oldest intensely cultivated areas on Earth. It is very heavily populated, with population densities up to 1,600 inhabitants per square kilometre. Deserts surround the low-lying, fertile floodplains. Only 2.5% of Egypt's land area, the Nile delta and the Nile valley, are suitable for intensive agriculture. Most of a 50km-wide land strip along the coast is less than 2m above sea level and is only protected from flooding by a 1–10km-wide coastal sand belt, shaped by discharge of the Rosetta and Damietta branches of the Nile. Erosion of the protective sand belt is a serious problem and has accelerated since the construction of the Aswan dam in the south of Egypt. A rising sea level would destroy weak parts of the sand belt, which are essential for the protection of lagoons and the low-lying reclaimed lands. These impacts could be very damaging. About one-third of Egypt's fish catches are made in the lagoons, and sea-level rise would change the water quality and affect most fresh-water fish; valuable agricultural land would be inundated; vital, low-lying installations in Alexandria and Port Said would be threatened; recreational tourism beach facilities would be endangered; and essential groundwater would be salinated. Many of these effects are preventable, as dykes and protective measures would stop the worst flooding up to a 50cm sea-level rise, though there may still be considerable groundwater salination and the impact of increasing wave action could be serious.

The most important influence on the impact of sea-level rise on coastal regions is the rate of change. At the moment, the predicted rise of about 50cm in the next 100 years can be dealt with if there is the economic foresight to plan for the protection and adaptation of coastal regions. This then comes back to the development of regional economies and the availability of resources to implement appropriate changes. If sea level rises by over 1m in the next 100 years, which is thought to be unlikely according to the IPCC, then humanity would doubtless have major problems adapting to it.

Storms and floods

Storms and floods are major natural hazards, and between 1951 and 1999 were responsible for 76% of the global insured losses, 58% of the economic loses, and 52% of fatalities from natural catastrophes. It is, therefore, essential we know what is likely to happen in the future. There is some evidence that the temperate regions, particularly in the northern hemisphere, have become more stormy over the last 50 years. The model simulations for the next 100 years for storms in mid-latitude regions differ widely. The computer models do, however, suggest that the proportion of rainfall occurring as heavy rainfall has and will continue to increase, as will the year-to-year variability. This will increase the frequency of flooding events.

Two-fifths of the world's population lives under the monsoon belt, which brings life-giving rains. Monsoons are driven by the temperature contrast between continents and oceans. For example, moisture-laden surface air blows from the Indian Ocean to the Asian continent and from the Atlantic Ocean into West Africa during northern hemisphere summers, when the land masses become much warmer than the adjacent ocean. In winter, the continents become colder than the adjacent oceans and high pressure develops at the surface, causing surface winds to blow towards the ocean. Climate models indicate an increase in the strength of the summer monsoons as a result of global warming over the next 100 years. There are three reasons to support why this should occur: (1) global warming will cause continents to warm more than the ocean in summer and this is the primary driving force of the monsoon system; (2) decreased snow cover on

Tibet, expected in a warmer world, will increase this temperature difference between land and sea, increasing the strength of the Asian summer; (3) warmer climate means the air can hold more water vapour, so the monsoon winds will be able to carry more moisture. For the Asian summer monsoon, this could mean an increase of 10–20% in average rainfall, with an inter-annual variability of 25–100% and a dramatic increase in the number of days with heavy rain. The most worrying model finding is the predicted increase in rain variability between years, which could double, making it very difficult to predict how much rainfall will occur each year – essential knowledge for farmers. An exception to this increase is given by the Met Office Hadley Centre GCM, which predicts reduced rainfall over Amazonia but increased rainfall in the other monsoon systems. This case study is discussed in more detail in the next chapter.

As we have seen in Chapter 3, there seems to be growing evidence that numbers of hurricanes and their intensity have increased over the last three decades in the North Atlantic and Western Pacific Oceans. Kerry Emanuel (MIT) and Peter Webster (Georgia Institute of Technology in Atlanta) and colleagues using different methods have demonstrated that the number and intensity of hurricanes are directly linked to the sea-surface temperature. So as global warming increases ocean temperatures, then it will become possible for more hurricanes to be spawned. But the effects of hurricanes on human society are not only related to their numbers or intensity, but rather whether they make landfall, and if they do, where.

For example, 1992 was a very quiet year for hurricanes in the North Atlantic Ocean. However, in August, one of the few hurricanes that year, Hurricane Andrew, hit the USA just north of Miami and caused damage estimated at $20 billion. In terms of where hurricanes hit in developed countries, the major effect is usually economic loss, while in developing countries the main effect is loss of life. For example, Hurricane Katrina, which hit New Orleans in 2005 (Figure 18), caused 1,500 deaths; Hurricane Mitch, which hit Central America, killed at least 25,000 people. Hurricane Katrina was not the worst storm that has hit the USA; a storm that hit Miami in 1926 was 150% larger but did little damage because Miami Beach was yet to be developed. In the USA, coastal population has doubled in the last 10 to 15 years. So in terms of climate change, therefore, mitigation policies will have little effect on the costs in the developed world, while adaptation of coastal regions will be essential. But in the developing world mitigation would have a large impact in reducing the total loss of life and preventing regional economic melt-down. For example, the immediate economic impact of Hurricane Katrina was over $150 billion, but its subsequent effect on the US economy was to boost it slightly, by 1%, that year due to the $105 billion injected by the Bush administration to help the reconstruction of the region. Compare this with Hurricane Mitch, which set back the economy of Central America by about a decade.

As can been seen from the case of Hurricane Katrina, storms and floods have the ability to destroy major cities. Many major cities around the world are vulnerable to flooding because they were built close to rivers or the coast to facilitate trade via the oceans. London is one such city. At the moment, London is protected from flooding by the Thames Barrier. The Thames Barrier was built in response to the catastrophic floods in 1953 and was finally ready for use in 1982 (it was officially opened on 8 May 1984). The Thames Barrier protects 150 square kilometres of London and property worth at least £80 billion. Because of the foresight of previous scientific advisors to the UK government, it was built to withstand a 1 in 2,000-year flood. With the increased sea level due to global warming, this risk by 2030 will increase to a 1 in 1,000-year event. For example, between 1982 and 2001 it was closed 63 times. In the winter 2000/1, it was closed 24 times. In 2003, the barrier was closed for 14 consecutive tides, and in November 2007 it was closed twice for a storm surge the same size

18. Hurricane Katrina devastated New Orleans in August 2005

as the one that occurred in 1953. At the moment, the UK economy is the fifth largest in the world, approximately £1.4 trillion per year generated through London. London is also one of the three main centres, along with New York and Tokyo, for 24-hour share-trading. If London were disabled by a major flood, then not only would this hit the economy of the UK, it potentially could disrupt global trade and precipitate a global recession. Hence, the UK Environment Agency has plans for significant sea-level rise into the future, including a prospective plan for a 4.5m rise.

Heat waves and droughts

As global temperatures increase, heat waves will increase. As precipitation becomes more unpredictable and is concentrated into more intense rainfall events, so drought will increase. Like storms and floods, heat waves and droughts are major killers. The 2003 heat wave in Europe killed an estimated 35,000 people (Figure 19). The people who die in heat waves are usually the elderly – medics call this 'harvesting', as these people were taken earlier than they would have normally died. The element that tends to kill the elderly is sustained night-time temperatures. Many of those 35,000 deaths were avoidable, either by designing homes to cool in the evening or by adding mechanical air-conditioning. This is why it is so difficult to understand the impacts of climate change as people and societies do start to adapt to new conditions. Figure 20 shows the 2003 European heat wave in the context of summer temperatures over the last 100 years and predicted for the next 100 years. What is clear is that the temperature of the 2003 heat wave will be the average summer temperature in 2050.

Droughts are also a major killer, because of a lack of fresh drinking water, and stagnant pools of water produce many diseases – interestingly, from a disease point of view, droughts are much worse than floods.

El Niño-Southern Oscillation

One of the most important and mysterious elements in global climate is the periodic switching of the direction and intensity of ocean currents and winds in the Pacific. Originally known as El Niño ('Christ child' in Spanish), as it usually appears at Christmas,

19. The 2003 European heat wave killed an estimated 35,000 people

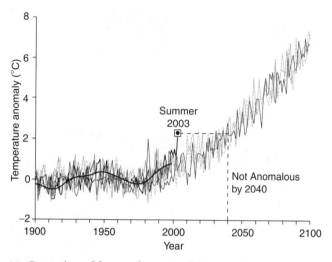

20. Comparison of the 2003 heat wave with past and future summer temperatures

and now more normally known as ENSO (El Niño–Southern Oscillation), this phenomenon typically occurs every three to seven years (Figure 21). It may last from several months to more than a year. The 1997–8 El Niño conditions were the strongest on record and caused droughts in the southern USA, East Africa, northern India, north-east Brazil, and Australia. In Indonesia, forest fires burned out of control in the very dry conditions. In California, parts of South America, Sri Lanka, and east-central Africa, there were torrential rains and terrible floods.

ENSO is an oscillation between three climates: the 'normal' conditions, La Niña, and 'El Niño'. El Niño conditions have been linked to changes in the monsoon, storm patterns, and occurrence of droughts all over the world. The state of the ENSO has also been linked to the position and occurrence of hurricanes in the Atlantic. For example, it is thought that the poor prediction of where Hurricane Mitch made landfall was because the ENSO conditions

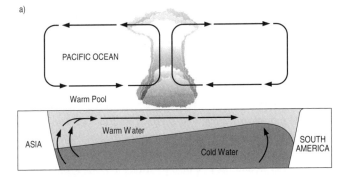

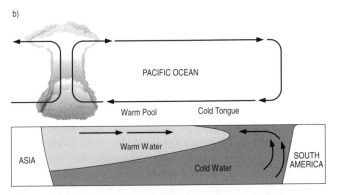

21. Description of the El Niño–Southern Oscillation: a) El Niño conditions, and b) La Niña conditions

were not considered and the strong trade winds helped drag the storm south across Central America instead of west as predicted.

Predicting El Niño events is very difficult but getting steadily easier. For example, there is now a large network of both ocean and satellite monitoring systems over the Pacific Ocean, primarily aimed at recording sea-surface temperature, which is the major indicator of the state of the ENSO. By using this climatic data in both computer circulation models and statistical models, predictions are made of the likelihood of an El Niño or La Niña event. We are really still in the infancy stage of developing our understanding and predictive capabilities of the ENSO phenomenon.

There is also considerable debate over whether ENSO has been affected by global warming. The El Niño conditions generally occur every three to seven years; however, in the last 20 years, they have behaved very strangely, returning for three years out of four: 1991–2, 1993–4, and 1994–5, then returning in 1997–8, but then they did not return for nine years, finally arriving in 2006–7. Reconstruction of past climate using coral reefs in the western Pacific shows sea-surface temperature variations dating back 150 years, well beyond our historical records. The sea-surface temperature shows the shifts in ocean current, which accompany shifts in the ENSO and reveal that there have been two major changes in the frequency and intensity of El Niño events. First was a shift at the beginning of the 20th century from a 10–15-year cycle to a 3–5-year cycle. The second was a sharp threshold in 1976 when a marked shift to more intense and even more frequent El Niño events occurred. These are sobering results considering the huge weather disruption and disasters caused by recent El Niño events. Modelling results also suggest that there could be a future 'heightened' state of El Niño which would permanently shift weather patterns. For example, it seems that the drought region in the USA could be shifting eastward. However, as we have seen, to predict an El Niño event six months from now is hard enough, without trying to assess whether or not ENSO is going to become more extreme over the next 100 years. Most computer models of ENSO in the future are inconclusive; some have found an increase and others have found no change. This is, therefore, one part of the climate system which we do not know how global warming will affect. Not only does ENSO have a direct impact on global climate but it also affects the numbers, intensity, and pathways of hurricanes and cyclones, and the strength and timing of the Asian monsoon. Hence, when discussing the potential impacts of global warming, one of the largest unknowns is the variation of ENSO and its knock-on effects on the rest of the global climate system.

Another possibility that we must consider is that in the early Holocene no evidence has been found for ENSO. In fact, it is thought that ENSO began some time between 4,000 and 5,000 years ago. Bjørn Lomborg radically suggests in his book *The Skeptical Environmentalist* that a 2–3°C warming could be a good thing for the future, as it may switch off ENSO. None of the computer models used to look at future climate has found this effect, and it must be remembered that the position of the Earth's orbit compared to the Sun was very different in the early Holocene, but it is something else to bear in mind.

Health

The potential health impacts of climate change are immense. Managing those health impacts is an enormous challenge, not simply an issue for health professionals, or indeed for climate change policy makers (see Figure 16). If we start with the basics, higher global temperatures will increase the death rate, which is usually measured in deaths per thousand people per year. For example 35,000 people died during the European heat wave of 2003. But care must be taken with these blanket assumptions as a recent study shows that the population in Europe can successfully make lifestyle adaptations to take into consideration the higher summer temperatures. This is a classic case of individual and local risk assessment and adaptation, because most heat-related mortality occurs when the temperature goes above an expected value. For example, in London heat-related mortality starts at 22.3°C, while in Athens it starts at 25.7°C. But the heat wave of 2003 shows that the population has not adapted to extreme events, which will be more common in the future.

Conversely, it has been suggested that the death rate may drop, since more people die from cold weather than warm weather, thus warmer winters would reduce this cause of death. However, this is a contested subject and no real consensus has yet emerged.

By far the most important threat to human health, however, is access to fresh drinking water. At present, rising human populations, particularly growing concentrations in urban areas, are putting great stress on water resources. The impacts of climate change – including changes in temperature, precipitation, and sea levels – are expected to have varying consequences for the availability of fresh water around the world. For example, changes in river run-off will affect the yields of rivers and reservoirs and thus the recharging of groundwater supplies. An increase in the rate of evaporation will also affect water supplies and contribute to the salinization of irrigated agricultural lands. Rising sea levels may result in saline intrusion in coastal aquifers. Currently, approximately 1.7 billion people, one-third of the world's population, live in countries that are water-stressed. IPCC reports suggest that with the projected global population increase and the expected climate change, assuming present consumption patterns, 5 billion people will experience water stress by 2025.

Climate change is likely to have the greatest impact in countries with a high ratio of relative use to available supply. Regions with abundant water supplies will get more than they want with increased flooding. As suggested above, computer models predict much heavier rains and thus major flood problems for Europe, whilst, paradoxically, countries that currently have little water (e.g. those relying on desalinization) may be relatively unaffected. It will be countries inbetween, which have no history or infrastructure for dealing with water shortages, that will be the most affected. In central Asia, North Africa, and southern Africa, there will be even less rainfall and water quality will become increasingly degraded through higher temperatures and pollutant run-off. Add to this the predicted increased year-to-year variability in rainfall, and droughts will become more common. Hence, it is those countries that have been identified as most at risk which need to start planning now to conserve their water supplies and/or deal with the increased risks of flooding, because it is the lack of infrastructure to deal with drought and floods rather than the lack or abundance of water which causes the threat to human health. Therefore, economic development of areas most at risk is essential in the next century to provide resources to mitigate the effects of global warming.

Another area where human health is threatened concerns access to and affordability of basic food. As was introduced at the beginning of this chapter, we are only now realizing how climate change policies can have negative effects on food availability. For example, increased oil prices, increased meat demand, and the recent rush to produce biofuels to mitigate global warming has contributed to food prices increases of 35%. The expansion of meat-eating in developing countries such as India and China is an important forcing factor, because beef cattle require 8kg of grain or meal for every kilogram of flesh they produce. Worryingly, these effects have combined to increase the cost of staples which much of the world relies upon just to stay alive: between March 2007 and March 2008, the price of corn increased by 31%, rice by 74%, soya by 87%, and wheat by 130%. This increase in food prices occurs at the same time that the global grain harvest of 2.1 billion tonnes in 2007 broke all previous records, being 5% higher than the previous year. Thus there is a huge mismatch between the use of grain for biofuels or as food. The amount of grain required to fill the tank of one car with ethanol could feed a person for a year. Riots, hunger, and starvation will be caused by policies trying to mitigate greenhouse gas emissions to deal with climate change. In addition, the drive for both biofuels and biodegradable plastics has accelerated deforestation in the tropics, increasing global warming, as countries and companies rush to plant palms and soya to make profit from this new market.

Another possible future threat to human health is the transmission of infectious diseases, as these are directly affected by climatic factors. Climate change will particularly influence vector-borne diseases (VBD), that is, diseases that are carried by another organism, as malaria is carried by mosquitoes. Infective agents and their vector organisms are sensitive to factors such as temperature, surface water, humidity, wind, soil moisture, and changes in forest distribution. It is, therefore, projected that climate change and altered weather patterns would affect the range (both altitude and latitude), intensity, and seasonality of many vector-borne and other infectious diseases. For example, there is a strong correlation between increased sea-surface temperature and sea level and the annual severity of the cholera epidemics in Bangladesh. With predicted future climate change and the rise in Bangladesh's relative sea level, cholera epidemics could become devastating.

In general, then, increased warmth and moisture caused by global warming will enhance transmission of diseases. But while the potential transmission of many of these diseases increases in response to climate change, we should remember that our capacity to control the diseases will also change. New or improved vaccination can be expected; some vector species can be constrained by use of pesticides. Nevertheless, there are uncertainties and risks here, too: for example, long-term pesticide use breeds resistant strains and kills many natural predators of pests.

The most important VBD is malaria, with currently 500 million infected people worldwide (about twice the population of the USA). *Plasmodium vivax*, which is carried by the *Anopheles* mosquito, is the organism that causes malaria. The main climate factors that have a bearing on the malarial transmission potential of the mosquito population are temperature and precipitation. Assessments of the potential impact of global climate change on the incidence of malaria suggest a widespread increase of risk because of the expansion of the areas suitable for malaria transmission. Mathematical models mapping out the suitable temperature zones for mosquitoes suggest that by the 2080s the potential exposure of people could increase by 2–4% (260–320 million people). The predicted increase is most pronounced at the borders of endemic malarial areas and at higher altitudes within malarial areas. The changes in malaria risk must be interpreted on the basis of local environmental conditions, the effects of socioeconomic development, and malaria control programmes or capabilities. The incidence of infection is most sensitive to climate changes in areas of South-East Asia, South America, and parts of Africa. Global warming will also provide excellent conditions for *Anopheles* mosquitoes to breed in southern England, continental Europe, and the northern USA.

It should, however, be noted that the occurrence of most tropical diseases is related to development. As recently as the 1940s, malaria was endemic in Finland, Poland, Russia, and 36 states in the USA including Washington, Oregon, Idaho, Montana, North Dakota, New York, Pennsylvania, and New Jersey. So although global warming has the potential to increase the range of many of these tropical diseases, the experience of Europe and the USA suggests that combating malaria is strongly linked to development and resources: development to ensure efficient monitoring of the disease and resources to secure a strong effort to eradicate the mosquitoes and their breeding grounds.

Biodiversity

The IPCC 2007 Impact report lists the following species as those most at risk from climate change as a result of global warming: the mountain gorilla in Africa; amphibians that live in the cloud forests of the neotropics; the spectacled bear of the Andes; forest birds of Tanzania; the 'resplendent quetzal' bird in Central America; the Bengal tiger, and other species found only in the Sundarban wetlands; rainfall-sensitive plants found only in the Cape Floral

Kingdom of South Africa; and polar bears and penguins near the poles. The primary reason for the threat to these species is that they are unable to migrate in response to climate change because of their particular geographical location or the encroachment of human activity, particularly farming and urbanization. An example of the former is the cloud forests of the neotropics: as climate changes, this particular climatic zone will migrate up the mountainside until the point where there is no more mountain.

One example of an ecosystem under threat is the coral reefs. Coral reefs are a valuable economic resource for fisheries, recreation, tourism, and coastal protection. Some estimate that the global cost of losing the coral reefs runs into hundreds of billions of dollars each year. In addition, reefs are one of the largest global stores of marine biodiversity. The last few years have seen unprecedented declines in the health of coral reefs. In 1998, El Niño was associated with record sea-surface temperatures and associated coral bleaching, which is when the coral expels the algae that live within it and that are necessary to its survival. In some regions, as much as 70% of the coral may have died in a single season. There has also been an upsurge in the variety, incidence, and virulence of coral disease in recent years, with major die-offs in Florida and much of the Caribbean region. In addition, increasing atmospheric carbon dioxide concentrations could decrease the calcification rates of the reef-building corals, resulting in weaker skeletons, reduced growth rates, and increased vulnerability to erosion. Model results suggest these effects would be most severe at the current margins of coral reef distribution.

On a more theoretical note, a recent study by Chris Thomas and colleagues (published in *Nature* in 2004) investigated the possible increase in the likely extinction rate over the next 50 years in key regions such as Mexico, Amazonia, and Australia. The theoretical models suggest that by 2050 the climatic changes predicted by the IPCC would commit 18% (warming of 0.8–1.7°C), 24%

(1.8–2.0°C), and 35% (above 2.0°C) of the species studied to extinction in these regions. That means one-quarter of all species in these regions may become extinct by the middle of this century. There are many assumptions in their models which may or may not be true; for example, they assume we know the full climatic range in which each species can persist and the precise relationship between shrinking habitat and extinction rates. So these results should be seen only as the likely direction of extinction rates, not necessarily the exact magnitude. However, these predictions do represent a huge future threat to regional and global biodiversity and illustrate the sensitivity of biological systems to the amount and rate of warming that will occur in the future.

Agriculture

One of the major worries concerning future climate change is the effect it will have on agriculture, both globally and regionally. The main question is whether the world can feed itself under the predicted future global warming conditions. Predictions of cereal production for 2060 suggest that there are still huge uncertainties about whether climate change will cause global agricultural production to increase or decrease. If the predicted temperature increases are considered, then we expect there to be a drop in food production in both the developed and less-developed countries. But if other effects are taken into consideration, then this effect of temperature is greatly reduced, or in the case of the developed world becomes an increase. One of the most important additional factors is that increased atmospheric carbon dioxide acts as a fertilizer; thus scientific studies have shown that plants in an atmosphere that contains more carbon dioxide grow faster and better, because the carbon dioxide is essential for photosynthesis and the prime source of carbon for plants. So plants like more atmospheric carbon dioxide, and thus farm yields may increase in the future in many regions.

In addition, if it is assumed that farmers can take action to adapt to changing climate, this also boosts or at least maintains agricultural production in many regions. For example, farmers could vary the planting time and/or switch to a different variety of the same plant to respond to changing conditions. Therefore, models suggest that with reasonable assumptions on a worldwide scale, the change is expected to be small or moderate. But this does not mean the amount of cereal produced worldwide will be the same or lower in 2060 compared with today. Since 1960, world grain production has doubled and is predicted to continue to rise at a similar rate. So even a pessimistic 1999 study using the Met Office Hadley Centre climate model estimated that cereal production in 2080 would increase by only 90% compared with today, not by 94% which would have occurred in the absence of global warming. However, as we have discussed in the Health section above, it is important to discuss how much of the land that would have been used for cereal production in the future may be used for biofuels or as feed for livestock. The question then becomes: is a 90% increase enough to feed an expanding global population, supply an increasing demand for biofuel, and keep pace with the increase in meat-eating around the world?

The general global trend, however, masks the huge changes that will occur regionally, with both winners and losers – the poorest countries, of course, which are least able to adapt, being the losers. Also, the results of all these studies are heavily dependent on the assumed trade models and market forces used, as, unfortunately, agricultural production in the world has very little to do with feeding the world's population and much more to do with trade and economics. This is why the European Union has stockpiles of food, while many underdeveloped countries export cash crops (such as sugar, cocoa, coffee, tea, and rubber) but cannot adequately feed their own populations. A classic example is the West African state of Benin, where cotton farmers can obtain cotton yields four to eight times per hectare greater than their US competitors in Texas. The USA subsidizes its farmers, however, which means that US cotton is cheaper than that coming from Benin. Currently, US cotton farmers receive \$3.9 billion in subsidies, almost twice the total GDP of Benin. So even if global warming makes Texan cotton yields even lower, it still does not change the biased market forces.

So in the computer models, markets can reinforce the difference between agricultural impacts in developed and developing countries and, depending on the trade model used, agricultural exporters may gain in monetary terms even though the supplies fall, because when a product becomes scarce, the price rises. The other completely unknown factor is the extent to which a country's agriculture can be adaptable. For example, the models assume that production levels in developing countries will fall to a greater degree compared with those in the developed countries because their estimated capability to adapt is less than that of developed countries. But this is just another assumption that has no analogue in the past, and as these effects on agriculture will occur over the next century, many developing countries may catch up with the developed world in terms of adaptability.

One example of the real regional problems that global warming could cause is the case of coffee-growing in Uganda. Here, the total area suitable for growing Robusta coffee would be dramatically reduced, to 10% of the present area, by a temperature increase of 2°C. Only higher areas of land would remain suitable for coffee; the rest would become too hot to grow coffee. But no one can tell whether these remaining areas would make more or less money for the country, because if other coffee-growing areas around the world are similarly affected, the price of coffee beans will increase due to scarcity. This demonstrates the vulnerability to the effects of global warming of many developing countries, whose economies often rely heavily on one or two agricultural products, as it is very difficult to predict the changes that global warming will cause in terms of crop yield and its cash equivalent. Hence, one major adaptation to global warming should be the broadening of the economic and agricultural base of the most threatened countries. This, of course, is much harder to accomplish in practice than on paper, and it is clear that the EU and US agricultural subsidies and the current one-sided World Trade Agreements have a greater effect on global agricultural production and the ability of countries to feed themselves than global warming will ever have. Solutions look even further away with the failure of the World Trade Organization negotiations which collapsed in 2008.

Summary

The impacts of global warming will increase significantly as the temperature of the planet rises. Warming will affect the return period and severity of floods, droughts, heat waves, and storms. Coastal cities and towns will be especially vulnerable as sea-level rise will worsen the effects of floods and storm surges. Water security, food security, and public health will become the most important problems facing all countries. Global warming threatens global biodiversity and the wellbeing of billions of people.

In Table 2, there is a summary of the effects of global warming given by the rise in global temperature, as far as 5–6°C. Even the IPCC has avoided discussing a world that hot. However, I think it is important for us to have an understanding of what this sort of climate change would mean to the planet to ensure we never go there. With sustained global temperatures of 5–6°C above present-day levels, both Greenland and the Western Antarctic ice sheet will have started to melt by the middle of next century. If these two ice sheets completely melt, sea level would rise by 13m. At the moment, the UK Environment Agency has plans to deal with a 4.5m rise in sea level which entail a huge barrier across the mouth of the River Thames, stretching from Essex to Kent. However, a sea-level rise of 13m would mean the flooding and permanent abandonment of nearly all lower-lying coastal and river urban areas. At the moment, one-third of the world's population lives within 60 miles of a shoreline and 13 of the world's 20 largest cities are located on a coast. This means billions of people could be displaced, starting environmental mass migration. The North Atlantic Ocean circulation would collapse, plunging Western Europe into a succession of severe winters which would be followed by severe heat waves every summer. At least 3 billion people in the world would become water-stressed. Agricultural production would start to fail, and billions of people would face starvation. Water and food security would become issues of conflict between countries, so that some experts are predicting 'eco-wars'. Public health systems around the world may collapse, unable to cope with the demands. Global biodiversity would be devastated. As I said: let's not go there.

Chapter 6
Surprises

All the impacts discussed above assume that there is a linear relationship between greenhouse gas forcing and climate change, as produced by the AOGCMs. There is, however, increasing concern among scientists that climate change may occur abruptly. This is because there is recent scientific evidence that many past climatic changes have occurred with startling speed. For example, ice-core records suggest that half the warming in Greenland since the last ice age was achieved in only a decade. Some of these regional changes involved temperature changes of over 10°C. This relates back to Chapter 1 and the discussion of how climate changes, whether it varies smoothly or contains thresholds and bifurcations. Such is the concern that future climate change may be abrupt that in 2003 the prestigious Royal Society in London convened a conference and published an associated report on this very topic, while the National Research Council (NRC) in the USA commissioned a report on *Abrupt Climate Change*, published in 2002. What both reports stress is the need for the wider community of natural and social scientists, as well as policymakers, to recognize the potential for climate to change abruptly and to act accordingly. The NRC report makes five recommendations:

1) Improve the fundamental knowledge base related to abrupt climate change.

Below, I review four possible abrupt climate surprises: melting of Greenland and/or Antarctica, deep-ocean circulation, gas hydrates, and Amazonia. But what connects them all is that we really do not know how the global climate will react to global warming in the future. It is thus essential for more work to be done on how abruptly these changes occur. Moreover, the NRC report suggests there is a need for greater understanding of how the global and regional economies would deal with abrupt climate change.

2) Improve modelling focused on abrupt climate change.

At the moment, most models try to achieve a steady-state or equilibrium between the forcing and the variations. What is required is a new type of high-resolution model to look at how easily abrupt climate change can occur. The NRC report stressed that new possible mechanisms of abrupt climate change should be investigated and a hierarchy of models will be required, since many of these abrupt changes are initiated at the fine spatial scale, which AOGCMs are currently unable to simulate.

3) Improve palaeoclimatic data related to abrupt climate change.

Past climate changes have provided us with many of the clues about how future climate could change. For example, oceanographers had not considered the idea that the deep-ocean circulation could change until it was shown that it was radically different during the last ice age. The NRC report suggests that improvement is required in both geographical and temporal resolution of abrupt events in the past. Also there is a need to focus on water, both too much (floods) and too little (droughts), as these are by far the most important influences on humanity.

4) Improve statistical approaches.

This has been mentioned before in this book, but current practice in climate statistics is to assume a simple unchanging distribution of outcomes. However, as we have seen in Figure 17, a one-in-30-year extreme event will statistically no longer occur once in 30 years. So the 'past as the key to the future' assumption leads to serious underestimation of the likelihood of extreme events; hence at the moment the conceptual basis and application of climate statistics is being re-examined using 'extreme value theory', particularly as all future predictions are that the year-to-year variability in extreme weather will increase in the future.

5) Investigate 'no-regrets' strategies to reduce vulnerability.

The NRC report stresses that research should be undertaken to identify 'no-regrets' measures to reduce vulnerabilities and increase adaptive capacity at little or no cost. No-regrets measures may include low-cost steps to slow climate change, improve climate forecasting, slow biodiversity loss, or improve water, land, and air quality. Technological changes, such as clean technology, may increase the adaptability and resilience of both economic and ecological systems faced with abrupt climate change. The report stresses the need for research into how poor countries can be assisted to develop a more adaptable scientific and economic infrastructure to reduce the effects of abrupt climate change.

Below, I discuss just four possible 'surprises' that could occur in the next 100 years because of global warming. What is common to all these hypotheses is that we really have no idea if and when they will happen and, if they do, what will be the effects.

Melting of Greenland and/or Antarctica

The estimates for sea-level rise for the next 100 years in the IPCC report of 2007 are lower than those in the IPCC 2001 report. The reason is that estimates of the possible contribution of ice flow were taken out, due to a lack of understanding. Ice-flow rates did increase between 1992 and 2003 in both Greenland and

Antarctica, but it is unknown whether this contribution will continue. If this contribution is linear with surface warming, then another 10cm to 20cm can be added to the sea-level estimates, giving a range of 28cm to 79cm by 2100, which is approximately the IPCC 2001 report estimate. But with another six years of study, scientists have realized that we do not know enough about Greenland and Antarctica. There is already a lot of evidence that they are starting to melt. For example, Greenland over the past four summers has lost between 380 and 490 billion tonnes of ice each year, which is about 150 billion tonnes more than it receives each winter in terms of snow.

Greenland and Antarctica constitute one of the most worrying potential climate surprises. If the large ice sheets there completely melted, their contribution to global sea-level rise would be as follows: Greenland, about 7m; West Antarctic ice sheet, about 8.5m; East Antarctic ice sheet, about 65m; compared with just 0.3m if all the mountain glaciers melted. Palaeoclimate data show that the huge East Antarctica ice sheet developed 35 million years ago due to the progressive tectonic isolation of Antarctica and that it has in fact remained stable in much warmer climates. However, scientists are now very worried that either Greenland or the West Antarctic could start to melt in the next 100 years. This would mean metres of global sea-level rise which would threaten all coastal populations of the world. There is also scientific debate about what happens to both the Greenland and Antarctic ice sheets beyond the next 100 years; even if significant melting does not occur this century, we may have started a process that causes irreversible melting during the next one.

Thus what happens in the next 100 years will determine the future of these ice sheets and the livelihoods of billions of people who live close the coast. What is obvious is that a great deal more research is required on the climatic history of Greenland and Antarctica and on monitoring changes that are occurring now.

Deep-ocean circulation

The circulation of the ocean is one of the major controls on our global climate. In fact, the deep ocean is the only candidate for driving and sustaining internal long-term climate change (of hundreds to thousands of years) because of its volume, heat capacity, and inertia. In the North Atlantic, the north-east trending Gulf Stream carries warm and salty surface water from the Gulf of Mexico up to the Nordic seas (Figure 22). The increased saltiness, or salinity, in the Gulf Stream is due to the huge amount of evaporation that occurs in the Caribbean, which removes moisture from the surface waters and concentrates the salts in the sea water. As the Gulf Stream flows northward, it cools down. The combination of a high salt content and low temperature makes the surface water heavier or denser. Hence, when it reaches the relatively fresh oceans north of Iceland, the surface water has cooled sufficiently to become dense enough to sink into the deep ocean. The 'pull' exerted by the sinking of this dense water mass helps maintain the strength of the warm Gulf Stream, ensuring a current of warm tropical water flowing into the north-east Atlantic, sending mild air masses across to the European continent. It has been calculated that the Gulf Stream delivers 27,000 times the energy of all of Britain's power stations put together. If you are in any doubt about how good the Gulf Stream is for the European climate, compare the winters at the same latitude on either side of the Atlantic Ocean, for example London with Labrador, or Lisbon with New York. Or a better comparison is between Western Europe and the west coast of North America, which have a similar geographical relationship between the ocean and continent – so think of Alaska and Scotland, which are at about the same latitude.

The newly formed deep water sinks to a depth of between 2,000m and 3,500m in the ocean and flows southward down the Atlantic Ocean, as the North Atlantic Deep Water (NADW). In the South Atlantic Ocean, it meets a second type of deep water, which is

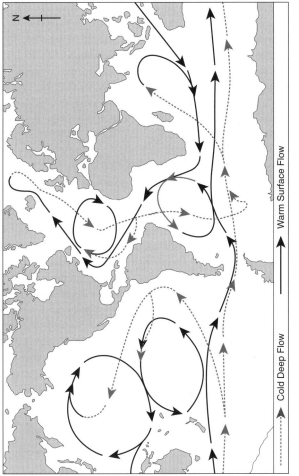

22. **The deep circulation of the ocean, termed the oceanic conveyor belt**

······▶ Cold Deep Flow   ───▶ Warm Surface Flow

formed in the Southern Ocean and is called the Antarctic Bottom Water (AABW). This is formed in a different way to NADW. Antarctica is surrounded by sea ice and deep water forms in coast polnyas, or large holes in the sea ice. Out-blowing Antarctic winds push sea ice away from the continental edge to produce these holes. The winds are so cold that they super-cool the exposed surface waters. This leads to more sea-ice formation and salt rejection, producing the coldest and saltiest water in the world. AABW flows around the Antarctic and penetrates the North Atlantic, flowing under the warmer, and thus somewhat lighter, NADW (Figure 23a). The AABW also flows into both the Indian and Pacific Oceans.

This balance between the NADW and AABW is extremely important in maintaining our present climate, as not only does it keep the Gulf Stream flowing past Europe, but it maintains the right amount of heat exchange between the northern and southern hemispheres. Scientists have shown that the circulation of deep water can be weakened or 'switched off' if there is sufficient input of fresh water to make the surface water too light to sink. This evidence has come from both computer models and the study of past climates. Scientists have coined the phrase 'dedensification' to mean the removal of density by adding fresh water and/or warming up the water, both of which prevent sea water from being dense enough to sink. As we have seen, there is already concern that global warming will cause significant melting of the polar ice caps. This will lead to more fresh water being added to the polar oceans. Global warming could, therefore, cause the collapse of NADW, and a weakening of the warm Gulf Stream (Figure 23b). This would cause much colder European winters and more severe weather. However, the influence of the warm Gulf Stream is mainly in the winter so it does not affect summer temperatures. So, if the Gulf Stream fails, global warming would still cause European summers to heat up. Europe would end up with extreme seasonal weather very similar to that of Alaska.

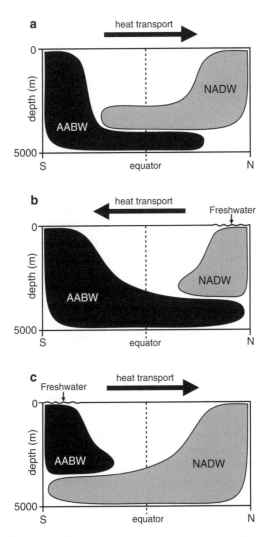

23. **Different possible circulation of the deep ocean depending on sea-surface salinity, that is fresh-water input**

A counter scenario is that if the Antarctic ice sheet starts to melt significantly before the Greenland and Arctic ice, things could be very different. If enough melt-water is put in the Southern Ocean, then AABW will be severely curtailed. Because the deep-water system is a balancing act between NADW and AABW, if AABW is reduced then the NADW will increase and expand (Figure 23c). The problem is that NADW is warmer than AABW, and because if you heat up a liquid it expands, the NADW will take up more space. So any increase in NADW will mean an increase in sea level. Computer models by Dan Seidov (previously at Pennsylvania State University) and myself have suggested that a melt-water event in the Southern Ocean could cause a reduction in the AABW and the expansion of the NADW, and would result in an average sea-level increase of 2m. The problem is that we have no idea how much fresh water it will take to shut off either the NADW or the AABW. Nor at the moment can we predict which will melt first, the Arctic or Antarctic. We do know that these events have happened frequently in the past and have drastically altered the global climate. If global warming continues, some time in the future enough melt-water will be generated and the options will be either severe alteration of the European climate or an additional 2.5m of global sea-level rise.

Not only do we not know how much fresh water is required to reduce either North Atlantic or Southern Ocean deep-water formation, we are also not sure whether it could be reversed. This is because computer models suggest the fresh-water–deep-ocean system could be a threshold-bifurcated system. Figure 24 demonstrates this bifurcation of the climate system and shows that there can be different relationships between climate and the forcing mechanism, depending on the direction of the threshold. The bifurcation system is very common in natural systems, for example in cases where inertia or the shift between different states of matter needs to be overcome. Figure 24 shows that in cases A and B the system is reversible, but in case C it is not. In case C, the control variable must increase to more than it was

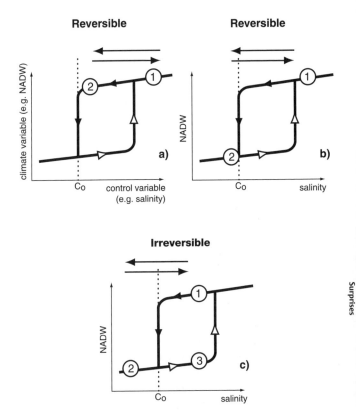

24. Bifurcation of the climate system

in the previous equilibrium state to get over the threshold and
return the system to its pre-threshold state. Let us consider this in
terms of the salinity of the North Atlantic versus the production of
North Atlantic Deep Water (NADW). We know that adding more
fresh water to the North Atlantic hampers the production of salty,
cold, and hence heavy deep water. In case A, changing the salinity
of the North Atlantic has no effect on the amount of NADW
produced. It is a very insensitive system. In case B, reducing the
salinity reduces the production of NADW; however, if the salt is

replaced, then the production of NADW returns to its previous, pre-threshold level.

In case C, reducing the North Atlantic salinity reduces the production of NADW. However, simply returning the same amount of salt does not return the NADW production to the normal level. Because of the bifurcation, a lot more salt has to be injected to bring back the NADW production to its previous level (see Figures 5e and 24c). It may be that the extra amount of salt required is not possible within the system and so this makes the system theoretically irreversible. The major problems we face when looking at future climate change is whether a bifurcation system exists and whether the system will go beyond a point of being reversible. What is worrying is that these threshold systems can apply to any part of the climate system. Another example is the position of the monsoons: in Oman and other parts of Arabia, fresh groundwater has been dated to 18,000 years ago, to the last ice age; none of it is any younger. This suggests that under glacial conditions the modern South-East Asian monsoon belt came much further north, producing significant rains in what are now extremely arid regions. As soon as the global climate moved into an interglacial, the monsoons shifted. The next question is: if global warming changes the position of the monsoons again, will they return to the present position if the effects of global warming lessen?

Gas hydrates

Currently, below the world's oceans and permafrost lurks a deadly threat – gas hydrates. These are a mixture of water and methane, which is sustained as a solid at very low temperatures and very high pressures. These gas hydrates are a solid composed of a cage of water molecules, which hold individual molecules of methane and other gases. The methane comes from decaying organic matter found deep in ocean sediments and in soils beneath permafrost. These gas hydrate reservoirs are extremely unstable, as a slight increase in temperature or decrease in pressure can cause them to destabilize. The impacts of global warming include the heating up of both the oceans and the permafrost, which could cause the gas hydrates to break down, pumping out huge amounts of methane into the atmosphere. Methane is a very strong greenhouse gas, 21 times more powerful than carbon dioxide. If enough were released, it would raise temperatures even more, releasing even more gas hydrates – producing a runaway greenhouse effect. Scientists really have no idea how much methane is stored in the gas hydrates beneath our feet: estimates are between 1,000 and 10,000 gigatonnes of gas hydrates, a huge range (compared with only 180 gigatonnes of carbon dioxide currently in the atmosphere). Without a more precise estimate, it is very difficult to assess the risk posed by gas hydrates.

The reason why scientists are so worried about this issue is because there is evidence that a super greenhouse effect occurred 55 million years ago, during what is called the Palaeocene–Eocene Thermal Maximum (PETM). During this hot-house event, scientists think that up to 1,500 gigatonnes of gas hydrates may have been released. This huge injection of methane into the atmosphere accelerated the natural greenhouse effect, producing an extra 5°C of warming. There is still, however, considerable debate over the PETM: for example, was it gas hydrate or volcanic carbon dioxide release that caused the warming? Scientists do not know whether global warming will cause a significant release of gas hydrates. We also do not know how the gas hydrate will react to climate change. It is clear that the gas hydrate stored in the permafrost will be released when the ice melts. However, the gas hydrate under the ocean is kept stable both by the high pressure and the low temperatures. As ocean temperatures change, this will be transmitted through the gas hydrate, causing some of it to melt, but if this process is slow enough, the gas released could migrate up in the ocean sediment and re-freeze at a higher level. So we have little idea whether future climate change could cause these so-called 'burps of death'.

There is another problem. If significant parts of the Greenland and Antarctic ice sheets melt, the removal of ice from the continent means that it will recover and start to move upwards. This isostatic rebound can be seen in the British Isles, which are still recovering from the last ice age, with Scotland still rising while England is sinking. This will mean that the relative sea level around the continental shelf will fall, removing the weight and thus the pressure of the sea water on the marine sediment. Pressure removal is a much more efficient way of destabilizing gas hydrates than temperature increases, and so huge amounts of methane could be released from around the Arctic and Antarctic.

There is another secondary effect of gas hydrate release: when the hydrates break down, they can do so explosively. There is clear evidence from the past that violent gas hydrate releases have caused massive slumping of the continental shelf and associated tsunamis (giant waves). The most famous is the Norwegian Storegga slide which occurred about 8,000 years ago, was the size of Wales, and produced a 15m-high tsunami that wiped out many prehistoric settlements in Scotland. In modern times, we have seen the 2004 Boxing Day tsunami in the Indian Ocean that killed more than 281,000 people. Hence, we cannot rule out the possibility that global warming could lead to an increased frequency of gas hydrate-generated submarine landslides and thus tsunamis of over 15m in height hitting our coasts. Up to now, only the countries around the Pacific rim are prepared for this type of tsunami event – but gas hydrate-generated tsunamis could occur anywhere in the ocean.

Amazonia

In 1542, Francisco de Orellana led the first European voyage down the Amazon River. During this intrepid voyage the expedition met a lot of resistance from the local Indians; in one particular tribe the women warriors were so fierce that they drove their male warriors in front of them with spears. Thus the river was named after the famous women warriors of the Greek myths, the Amazons. This makes Francisco de Orellana one of the unluckiest explorers of that age, as normally the river would have been named after him. This voyage also inspired our almost mystical wonder about the greatest river and the largest area of rainforest in the world, something we still feel today.

The Amazon River discharges approximately 20% of all fresh water carried to the oceans. The Amazon drainage basin is the world's largest, covering an area of 7,050,000 square kilometres, about the size of Europe. The river is a product of the Amazon monsoon, which every summer brings huge rains. This also produces the spectacular expanse of rainforest, which supports the greatest diversity and largest number of species of any area in the world. The Amazon rainforest is also important when it comes to the future of global warming, as it is a huge natural store of carbon. Up until recently, it was thought that an established rainforest such as the Amazon had reached maturity and thus could not take up any more carbon dioxide. Experiments in the heart of the Amazon rainforest have shown this could be wrong and that the Amazon rainforest might be sucking up an additional 5 tonnes of atmospheric carbon dioxide per hectare per year. This is because plants react favourably to increased carbon dioxide; because it is the raw material for photosynthesis, the more of it the better. So having more carbon dioxide in the atmosphere acts like a fertilizer, stimulating plant growth. Because of the size of the Amazon rainforest, it seems that presently it is taking up a large percentage of our atmospheric carbon dioxide pollution, about three-quarters of the world's car pollution. But things could change in the future.

Global climate models developed at the Met Office Hadley Centre suggest that global warming by 2050 could have increased the winter dry season in Amazonia. For the Amazon rainforest to survive, it requires not only a large amount of rain during the wet season but a relatively short dry season so that it does not dry out.

According to the Hadley Centre model, global warming could cause the global climate to shift towards a more El Niño-like state with a much longer South American dry season. Kim Stanley Robinson in his novel *Forty Signs of Rain* uses the term 'Hyperniño' to refer to a new climate state. Hence, the Amazon rainforest could no longer survive and would be replaced by savannah (dry grassland), which is found both to the east and south of the Amazon basin today. This replacement would occur because the extended dry periods would lead to forest fires destroying large parts of the rainforest. This would also return the carbon stored in the rainforest back into the atmosphere, accelerating global warming. The savannah would then take over those burnt areas, as it is adapted to coping with the long dry season, but savannah has a much lower carbon storage potential per square kilometre than rainforest. So the Amazon rainforest at the moment might be helping to reduce the amount of pollution we put into the atmosphere, but ultimately it may cause global warming to accelerate at an unprecedented and currently unpredicted rate (Figure 25).

However, we must still view this result with caution as not all models agree with the Met Office Hadley Centre results. This intercomparison is being carried out by the C^4MIP (more fully, Coupled Carbon Cycle Climate Model Intercomparison Project). It is a model intercomparison project along the lines of the Atmospheric Model Intercomparison Project, but for global climate models that include an interactive carbon cycle. The inclusion of an interactive carbon cycle is an extremely important step forward in climate models as ecologists have known for a long time that different vegetation types modify the local environment. This is especially true of the Amazon rainforest, which recycles at least 50% of the precipitation, maintaining a warm, moist environment.

The findings of the Met Office Hadley Centre model are dependent on the world moving to a more El Niño-like state;

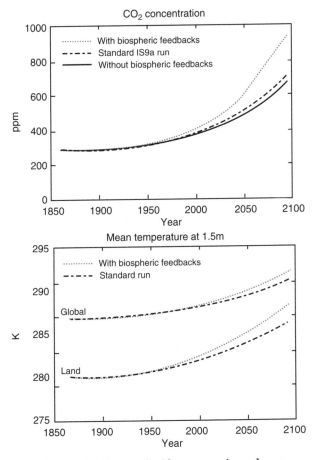

25. Met Office model of carbon dioxide concentration and mean temperature over time

many other GCMs show this trend, but not all. As the shift towards a more El Niño-like state is the key control on the future of the rainforest, it is something we need to have confidence in. As discussed earlier, confidence in science moves forward as a consequence of the weight of evidence, and at the moment there is not enough convincing evidence that the world will move into a more El Niño-like state, or Robinson's 'Hyperniño'. The dire prediction of the Met Office model does not just concern Amazonia, as 80% of the release of additional carbon from the terrestrial biosphere into the atmosphere comes from increased soil decomposition, which is a poorly understood process on the global scale. So the work of the C^4MIP is essential if we are to have any confidence concerning the future of the Amazon rainforest and global soil carbon.

Summary

Until a few decades ago, it was generally thought that significant large-scale global and regional climate changes occurred gradually over many centuries or millennia, hence the climate shifts were assumed to be scarcely perceptible during a human lifetime. We now know that human-induced climate change will radically affect the planet over the next 100 years. In addition, there may be potential surprises in the global climate system, exacerbating future climate change. As discussed above, these include the very real possibility that Greenland and/or the Antarctic could melt, raising sea level by metres. Or the North Atlantic-driven deep-ocean circulation could change, producing extreme seasonal weather in Europe. The Amazon rainforest could be burned in the future, accelerating global warming and destroying biodiversity. Finally, there is the unquantified threat of gas hydrates lurking beneath the oceans which could be released in 'giant burps of death' if the oceans warm up sufficiently – again, accelerating global warming.

So what effects could climate change have on human society? We know that abrupt past climate changes had profound effects on human history. For example, a short, cold, arid period about 4,300 years ago caused the collapse of classical civilizations around the world, including the Old Kingdom in Egypt; the Akkadian Empire in Mesopotamia; the Early Bronze Age societies of Anatolia,

Greece, and Israel; the Indus valley civilization in India; the Hilmand civilization in Afghanistan; and the Hongshan culture of China. It has also been shown that climate deterioration, particularly a succession of severe droughts in Central America during the Medieval Cold Period, prompted the collapse of the classic period of the Mayan civilization. Moreover, the rise and fall of the Incas can be linked to alternating wet and dry periods, which favoured the coastal and highland cultures of Ecuador and Peru.

We know, however, that humans can survive a whole range of climates. The collapse of these urban civilizations, then, is not simply about climate shifts making an area inhospitable; rather, the society was unable to adapt to the climate changes, particularly changes in water resources. For example, for the Mayan civilization to have survived, it would have needed to recognize its vulnerability to long-term water shortages and to have developed a more flexible approach, such as finding new water sources, developing new means of conserving water, and prioritizing water use in times of shortage. Hence the next two chapters are concerned with the global human response to climate change and a discussion of potential solutions, including how to ensure our civilization becomes flexible enough to deal with the possibility of climate surprises.

Chapter 7
Politics

The most logical approach to the global warming problem would be to cut emissions significantly. At the moment, many countries are developing very rapidly and thus global emissions are expanding at a faster and faster rate. So how much do we need to cut emissions by? As we have seen in previous chapters, scientists feel that 2°C is the tipping point when almost all people in the world become losers from climate change. So limiting climate change to 2°C seems to be the logical thing to do. Especially as the Stern Report in 2007 suggested the cost of adapting to a low-carbon economy now would be about 1% of world GDP, compared to costs of up to 20% world GDP if we do nothing. To try to limit climate change to 2°C, we need to understand how much carbon dioxide and other greenhouse gases that represents. Figure 26 shows the probability of temperature changes based on different amounts of atmospheric carbon dioxide. Even at the lowest level of 450ppm, there is at least a 40% chance that climate change will be above 2°C. Remember at the moment we are already at 379ppm and increasing at over 3% per year. So we face a huge challenge if we are to contain climate change to 2°C, and the only way we will do that is by a global binding agreement to cut emissions.

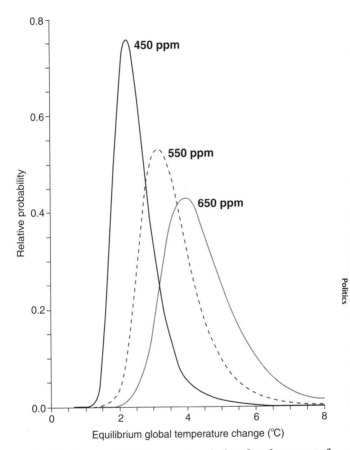

26. Predicted range of global temperature rise based on the amount of carbon dioxide in the atmosphere

Kyoto Protocol

So how are we doing on getting a global agreement to cut emissions of greenhouse gases? The United Nations Framework Convention on Climate Change (UNFCCC) was created at the Rio Earth Summit in 1992 to try to negotiate a worldwide agreement

Table 3. Comparison of selected countries' Kyoto Protocol legal target and their 2004 emissions

	Changes in emissions 1990–2004	
	Kyoto	2004
Australia	+8.0	+25.1
Italy	−6.5	+12.1
EU	−8.0	−0.6
Japan	−6.0	+6.5
Russia	0.0	−32.0
UK	−12.5	−14.3
USA	−7.0	+15.8

for reducing greenhouse gases and limiting the impact of global warming. Two major steps forward have been achieved in the last ten years. The first occurred at midnight on 13 December 1997, when the Kyoto Protocol was drawn up. This stated the general principles for a worldwide treaty on cutting greenhouse emissions and, more specifically, that all developed nations would aim to cut their emissions by 5.2% on their 1990 levels by 2008–12. However, some countries have continued to increase their emissions significantly since 1990 and thus will have great difficulty in achieving this overall reduction (see Table 3 for examples). The second breakthrough was in Bonn on 23 July 2001, when the Kyoto Protocol was ratified and signed, making it a legal treaty. However, the USA, under the leadership of President Bush, withdrew from the climate negotiations in March 2001 and so did not sign the Kyoto Protocol at the Bonn meeting. With the USA producing about one-quarter of the world's carbon dioxide pollution, this was a big blow for the treaty. Moreover, the targets set by the Kyoto Protocol were reduced during the Bonn meeting to make sure that Japan, Canada, and Australia would join. Australia finally made the Kyoto Protocol legally binding in December 2007. The targets for the 38 richest and most developed countries will be a cut of 1–3% compared with their 1990 levels.

The treaty does not include developing countries. This is a concern, because if countries such as India and China continue to develop, they will produce huge amounts of pollution. For example, if these two countries achieve their aim to have the same car to family ratio as Europe, there will be an extra billion cars in the world. The Kyoto Protocol entered into force on 16 February 2005. It could only come into effect after Russia ratified the treaty, thereby meeting the requirement that at least 55 countries, representing more than 55% of the global emissions made, signed up to it. Russia's membership tipped the scales, and allowed the Kyoto Protocol to become international law.

So what have the 186 nations signed up for? The 38 industrialized nations have agreed to binding targets to reduce their greenhouse gas emissions. The EU has turned the treaty into law for all member countries, forcing a cut in greenhouse gas emissions of 8% on the 1990 level by 2012. The United Kingdom's legal target is 12.5%, a larger reduction to allow poorer EU countries room for development. A total of $500 million (£350 million) new funds a year has been provided by the industrialized world to help developing countries to adapt to climate change and to provide new clean technologies. Industrial countries are also able to plant forests, manage existing ones, and change farming practices, and thereby claim credit for removing carbon dioxide from the atmosphere. In addition, there is provision in the Kyoto Protocol concerning national and international trade in carbon emissions. Currently, countries that have emission targets will be able to trade carbon emissions within their own national economy and between each other. This may be the only way that certain industrial countries make their cuts (see Table 3), and most will have to buy credits from Russia, whose greenhouse gas production dropped with the collapse of industry on the fall of communism. What has not yet been agreed is international trading with countries without emissions targets, as this was initially opposed by the EU and international environmental NGOs, but generally supported by other industrial nations and the less-developed world. There are many who want the Kyoto Protocol to go further and allow industrial nations to buy carbon credits from less-developed nations, and this is discussed later in the post-2012 agenda. At the moment, the Clean Development Mechanism (CDM) is the only way that developed countries can invest in and gain from a carbon credit in a developing country.

The main contenders

Below is a 'who's who' guide to the international climate talks. These different coalitions, which have formed during the climate change negotiations, provide us with some insight into the differing agendas of different countries. In addition, there are strong lobbying interests from both individual states and environmental, business, and industrial groups, which are also discussed below.

G-77 and China

The Group of 77 is the main developing country coalition and was formed in 1964 during the New International Economic Order negotiations under the UN Conference on Trade and Development (UNCTAD). China regularly allies itself with this group, which now numbers over 130 members. The country holding the annually rotating Chair of the Group 77 in New York serves as the Chair of the G-77 on climate change. During some of the Kyoto Protocol negotiations, the Chairs of the G-77 were: the Philippines (1995); Costa Rica (1996); and the United Republic of Tanzania (1997). The Group operates according to a consensus rule. Without consensus, that is all countries within this group agreeing, no common position is articulated. Given the wide variety of interests that the G-77 encompasses, however, it has been common for individual parties and groups also to speak during the Kyoto Protocol negotiations, even when there was a common position. G-77 symbolizes the North–South divide, with G-77 seeing climate change as essentially an issue about development. Two major concerns are expressed by this group: first, that poor countries' development will be hindered by having to reduce emissions; and second, that carbon trading must be allowed as a way of boosting income to developing countries.

AOSIS

The Alliance of Small Island States was formed in 1990 during the Second World Climate Conference to represent the interests of low-lying and small island countries that are particularly vulnerable to sea-level rise. It comprises some 43 states, most of which are also members of the G-77. This group has regularly spoken at the Protocol negotiations, often but not always through its Chair (Samoa, for most of the negotiations), though individual countries also intervened. The AOSIS position has always been to achieve the tightest control on global emissions, as their countries seem to be most at threat from the impacts of global warming.

JUSSCANNZ

This group of non-EU OECD (Organization for Economic Cooperation and Development) countries acted as a loose information-sharing coalition during the Kyoto Protocol negotiations, lacking coordinated positions. JUSSCANNZ stands for Japan, USA (who subsequently left the negotiations), Switzerland, Canada, Australia, Norway, and New Zealand. Iceland and other OECD countries, such as Mexico, often attended group meetings. The over-arching concern of JUSSCANNZ has always been the cost of tackling climate change. The group is, however, split. Japan, New Zealand, Norway, and Iceland already enjoy a high energy efficiency and/or an energy mix dominated by low-carbon sources. The greenhouse gas emissions per unit of GDP and per capita are, therefore, much lower than the OECD average, so their main concern is the cost of abatement. The second group is Australia, Canada, and the USA – the so-called 'New World' countries – who face very different national circumstances with relatively low energy efficiency and an energy mix dominated by fossil fuels, growing populations, and large geographical areas, all of which lead to high emissions per unit of GDP and per capita. These countries' main concern is the cost of mitigating climate change because of the cost of changing their energy-intensive infrastructure.

EU

The European Union has maintained a coordinated position on climate change, usually speaking through its presidency, which rotates every six months. For example, during the Protocol negotiations the following countries have presided over the EU: Spain (late 1995), France (early 1996), Ireland (late 1996), the Netherlands (early 1997), and Luxembourg (late 1997). It has been rare for individual EU states to speak during the Kyoto Protocol negotiations. The EU has a very similar split in its members to JUSSCANNZ, with both high and low energy-efficient economies. The consensus view of the EU has been to position itself as the environmental leader, with the attempt to advocate cuts as high as 15%. The EU rationale has been that any negotiated reduction could then be apportioned between the EU countries, depending on their development. This position has been greatly aided by both the UK and Germany experiencing a significant downturn in greenhouse emissions. In the UK, this was done by replacing coal with gas, while Germany's downturn was due to updating and cleaning up the inefficient industries of former East Germany. However, the internal divisions within the EU and its cumbersome internal decision-making procedures make it a frustrating negotiating partner.

OPEC

OPEC, the Organization of Petroleum Exporting Countries, regularly informally coordinated their positions in the climate change negotiations but have never spoken as a united group. The central position of this group is the protection of their main economic export, oil, and prevention of any treaty that undermines the significant usage of fossil fuels.

African Group

The African Group is a formal regional group under the UN system, but it has only sometimes intervened during the negotiations. More often, countries within this group have spoken for themselves or through the coordinating role of the G-77. The African Group has been used mainly for ceremonial statements.

ENGOs

ENGOs is short for Environmental Non-Governmental Organizations and, though not homogeneous, they had a relatively united view on climate change. They universally accepted the science of climate change and its possible impact, and campaigned for strong commitments on the part of governments and business to address the problem. However, there are significant differences among the ENGOs regarding specific issues in the negotiations, particularly the possibility of emissions trading. The split can be seen in terms of reflecting a cultural difference between the New and Old Worlds. For example, Greenpeace International, based in Amsterdam, is strongly opposed to emissions trading, while Brazilian Friends of the Earth are strongly supportive of it.

BINGOs

Business and Industry Non-Governmental Organizations (BINGOs) were another powerful lobby at the Kyoto Protocol negotiations. However, unlike the ENGOs, they are a diverse and loose-knit group, with three main sub-groups. At the more progressive end of the spectrum lie 'green' business, including the 'sunrise' renewable energy industries and insurance companies, who recognized climate change as a potential business opportunity and urged decisive action on the part of governments. The middle ground was occupied by a group which accepted the science of climate change but called for a prudent, cautious approach to mitigation. At the other extreme are the fossil-fuel, mostly US-based industries such as the Global Climate Coalition. These were known as the grey BINGOs or the carbon club, who supported only the weakest action on climate change, stressing the economic costs and scientific uncertainties, echoing the editorials and by-lines of most US newspapers and the British *Times* (see Chapter 2). Some of these BINGOs openly opposed the negotiations. Most notable was the Climate Council, a US-based lobby group run by Don Pearlman, a partner in a Washington law firm, which is widely believed to be a front for the fossil-fuel and energy interests in the USA. They have worked with OPEC states to block progress in both the IPCC and the climate change negotiations.

Kyoto management

It is interesting that, despite all these different views and the size and the ambition of the talks, a study by Joanna Depledge at University College London showed that management of the Kyoto Protocol negotiations was effective. She also provides some key lessons that could be used to increase the effectiveness of multilateral negotiations and ensure that the process is strengthened as it continues into the future. These include the importance of having a single strong and efficient presiding officer or negotiation chair and secretariat team throughout the negotiating process, as these promote unity and continuity. A balance between procedural equity/transparency and efficiency must be maintained, because the negotiating process must always continue to move forward, but at the same time the participants must feel that it is a fair process. Bargaining and cooperation should be promoted to accelerate the negotiations and to prevent the tendency for discussion to stagnate. There must also be strategies to overcome procedural obstructions, as these are sometimes used as a stalling mechanism in negotiations. Finally, Depledge suggests that an institutional memory should be developed so that continued future negotiations have knowledge of what has and has not worked in the past.

Is the Kyoto Protocol flawed?

A. Not far enough

The first major flaw in the Kyoto Protocol, according to many, is that it does not go far enough. The Kyoto Protocol as currently negotiated has emissions cuts relative to 1990 levels of between 1% and 8% for just over half the developed world, with no restrictions for the less-developed world. Compare this with scientists' suggestion that up to a 60% global cut is required to prevent major climatic change. If room is left for development, it would mean that the developed world would have to cut emissions by at least 80% very soon because if the International Energy

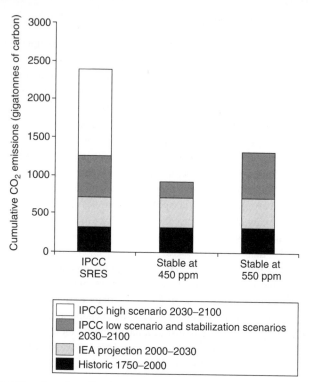

27. Historic and predicted global carbon dioxide emissions

Authority's projections are correct, then between 2000 and 2030 we will emit more carbon dioxide than during the whole of the historic period since 1750 (Figure 27). Hence many critics argue that the Kyoto Protocol will do nothing to prevent global warming and is not significantly different from a business-as-usual situation – which is of course what many developed countries want in order to maintain their economies (see Figure 28).

B. No enforcement

At the moment, very few countries are on the way to make their 2012 cuts negotiated in the Kyoto Protocol (see Table 3).

Even the EU, despite the very positive cuts in German and UK emissions, is not on target for the 8% cut. One way out will be to buy credits from Russia, the only major country to have made large cuts due to the collapse of its industrial production in the 1990s. But no one knows how much Russia will charge, nor how much its credits are really worth. However, if countries do not make their targets and do not buy credits, there is no enforcement beyond adding their failure to their next target. This is the huge problem with all international agreements: how do you sanction countries that sign up and do not comply? Because the first thing they can do is just drop out of the agreement. Novel ways of enforcing compliance at the international level must be found, otherwise there will always be those countries who cheat the system.

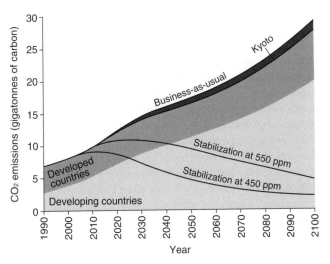

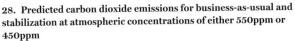

28. **Predicted carbon dioxide emissions for business-as-usual and stabilization at atmospheric concentrations of either 550ppm or 450ppm**

C. No USA

What even the most effective negotiations cannot deal with is withdrawal from the process. So the second major flaw in the Kyoto Protocol is the non-participation of the USA. It is, however, unsurprising that the USA withdrew from these climate change negotiations: US carbon dioxide emissions have already risen by 12% compared with 1990 levels and they are predicted to rise by more than 30% by 2012 compared to 1990 levels. So if they had agreed to ratify the Kyoto Protocol, they would have had to cut their emissions by over one-third, which successive presidents have seen as a direct threat to the US economy and thus their chances of re-election. As global carbon trading was not included in the Kyoto Protocol, so the USA did not have the possibility of trading their way to lower emissions. This, as we will see, is another fundamental flaw in the Kyoto Protocol that will have to be fixed in the post-2012 agreement.

There is, however, a deeper divide between the USA and, for example, the EU. Many political commentators have referred to this as the 'transatlantic rift'. Americans have historically tended not to see any source of democratic legitimacy higher than the constitutional nation-state. Therefore, any international organization has legitimacy only because the democratic majorities have handed up this legitimacy through a negotiated contractual process. Such legitimacy can be withdrawn at any time by the contracting parties. Europeans, by contrast, tend to believe democratic legitimacy flows from the will of an international community which is much larger than any individual nation-state. This international community hands down legitimacy to existing international institutions, which are seen as partially embodying the ideals and precepts of the international community.

At the start of the 21st century, the difference in approaches between the USA and other nation-states could not be more stark. Not only has the Bush administration withdrawn from the Kyoto

Protocol negotiations, but it has failed to ratify the Rio pact on biodiversity, withdrawn from the anti-ballistic missile treaty, opposed the ban on landmines, opposed amendments to the biological warfare convention, opposed the setting up of an international criminal court, and sidelined the UN in the lead-up to the second Iraq war. This pattern of US unilateralism should not be seen as merely a transitory problem reflecting the Bush administration, but rather it shows the fundamental schism between the worldviews of the USA and the rest of the Western world. This is not to say that either view is more or less valid. The problem is that 'future climate change' is a global concern, with causes and effects that go far beyond the boundaries of nation-states. Rather like the revolution in the 1980s, when the geographical scope of environmental problems was enlarged to encompass the globe, a new 'global' geographical view of politics is required. Hence the climate change negotiations and related world trade talks are fundamentally flawed without the multilateral, multi-nation-state approach. The USA is so important to both processes because of its economic size. Currently, the US population is ~300 million and has a GDP of $13 trillion, compared with the EU, which contains 490 million people and has a GDP of $15 trillion.

D. Green colonialism

Many social and political scientists have raised philosophical and ethical doubts about the entire Kyoto Protocol and the future direction of the climate negotiations. The main concern is that they reflect a version of colonialism, since rich developed countries are seen to be dictating to poorer countries how and when they should develop. Countries such as India and China have resisted calls to cut their emissions, stating that it would hurt their development and their mission to alleviate poverty. Others have, however, suggested that the Kyoto Protocol provides a development dividend via the Clean Development Mechanism

(CDM), because the CDM potentially provides a means by which money moves from the rich to the poorer countries. Again, however, all is not what it seems, as 80% of the project credits are in China, Brazil, India, and Korea, some of the richer developing countries, so funding is not perhaps being transferred to the poorest people in the world. Also, 60% of the carbon credits have been purchased by the UK and the Netherlands, resulting in a very skewed financial exchange.

The moral high ground of supposedly anti-green colonialism was also employed by the EU and international NGOs during the Kyoto Protocol process to block the suggestion of global carbon trading. They felt that those who had polluted most should cut first. However, national NGOs such as Greenpeace Brazil, developing countries, and the USA argued strongly that global carbon trading was the only way forward to ensure everyone signed up to the Kyoto Protocol. As we know, the moral high ground won and only CDMs were included. What is interesting is that the EU then realized it could not cut its own emissions the traditional way and thus set up the European Trading Scheme (ETS) for all facilities above 20 megawatts in the electricity, ferrous metals, cement, refineries, pulp and paper, and glass industries, which together represent over 40% of the EU total emissions. So with the success of the second phase of the ETS, we have a potential model for the next phase of the Kyoto Protocol.

E. Focus on the largest emitters

It has been argued that the assumption that emission mitigation is a global common problem is false. The idea that more than 170 countries need to agree to the Kyoto Protocol is symbolic but not practical when in reality fewer than 20 countries produce at least 80% of the world's emissions. Gwyn Prins (LSE) and Steve Rayner (Oxford) in the journal *Nature* in 2007 argue this point, and suggest that the other 150 countries just get in the way and slow the whole negotiation process down. There is some official realization of this, and in 2006 the G8+5 climate change dialogue was established to bring the 13 biggest polluters together for key discussions.

F. Nation verses sector approach

The Kyoto Protocol faces one other problem, which is embedded in the concept of the nation-state and is a major issue in a global capitalist world with supposedly free trade. For example, the USA has decided to sign the Kyoto Protocol and wants to reduce carbon emissions from heavy industry, so it imposes a carbon tax on steel and concrete production. However, other countries in the world do not have this restriction, so their products are cheaper even though they must be transported by ship, air, or road to the USA, emitting more carbon dioxide overall. So global economics can undermine any country trying to do the right thing and reduce their national emissions. An alternative approach is for global agreements to be made at the sector level. For example, there could be a global agreement on how much carbon can be emitted per ton of steel or concrete produced. All countries could then agree only to buy steel or concrete that is thus validated. This makes for a fairer trading scheme, and countries will not lose out if they adapt their industries to lower greenhouse gas emissions. The problems are, of course, how to police such a scheme across so many different industrial sectors.

Unilateral approach

With the realization that the Kyoto Protocol does not go far enough, a number of countries and regions have proposed carbon cuts way above those currently negotiated. For example, the United Kingdom now has a national law that binds the UK government to reduce the country's carbon emissions by 60% by 2050. They have set up a Climate Change Committee, independent of government, to monitor and advise successive governments on achieving this impressive goal. In fact in October 2008 they recommended that the target was raised to 80%. This

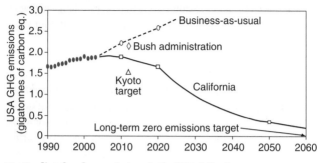

29. Predicted carbon emissions in the USA following a business-as-usual or California model

shows international independent leadership, because if the world's fifth largest economy can do it, then it is possible for other countries to follow. This same aim of a 60% reduction by 2050 has also been accepted into Californian State law. This may be very significant, as there is a history of innovative environmental laws in California being accepted as Federal laws in due course. If the California model were adopted by the whole of the USA, then this would make a huge difference to global emissions. This pathway is shown for comparison in Figure 29.

Other regions have shorter-term proposals. The EU Council of Ministers are proposing that after 2012 the EU should have a 20:20:20 aim by 2020: that is, 20% renewable energy for all 27 EU countries; 20% improvement in energy efficiency; and a 20% cut in total greenhouse gases if there is no global agreement, or 30% with a global agreement. So there are some very exciting political moves happening, way beyond the vision of the Kyoto Protocol.

Post-2012 agreement

The most important global political question of this century is what happens after 2012 when the Kyoto Protocol comes to an end. If we are to have any hope of dealing with global warming, we need a brave and farsighted post-2012 agreement. This will have to have a number of key conditions.

1) Contraction and convergence

The principle of contraction and convergence should be enshrined in the post-2012 agreement. This is the idea that the largest emitters of greenhouse gases contract the amount of pollution towards a designated per capita emissions total. For example, at the moment in the USA each person emits 10 times more carbon dioxide than a person in China. For global equality, the amount emitted per person should be the same. However, to do this and to ensure we keep climate change to a minimum, every country has to contract their emissions, some by a lot more than others. In the developed world, to ensure that other countries can develop as rapidly as possible policymakers must consider an ultimate zero-carbon budget for their country. Some countries who can export renewable or alternative energy may even be able to produce a negative carbon economy.

2) Developing world

The developing world must be involved and legally bound by the post-2012 agreement. First, they must be involved to enact the principle of contraction and convergence. Second, they must participate because during the rest of the 21st century most of the increase in greenhouse gas emissions will be from the developing world (see Figure 29). Even if the developed world reduced its emissions to zero tomorrow, by 2030 global emissions would be above today's level. This does not mean that economic development nor poverty alleviation should be adversely affected.

3) Global carbon trading

Global carbon trading must now become part of the international agreement on climate change. At the moment, only Annex 1 countries (the developed world) in the Kyoto Protocol can trade carbon. As you can see from Table 3, the collapse of the Russian economy in the 1990s means it has lots of spare credits to help other countries meet their 2012 obligations – the question will be how much will they charge. However, the developing world has been left out, and to fulfil points 1 and 2 above they must be involved.

The most successful system of carbon trading is 'cap and trade', whereby politicians set a cap, a maximum total of pollution allowed, and a trading system is then set up so that the different industries can trade credits. It is acknowledged that different industries can clean up at different rates and at different costs, and this trading system allows the most cost-effective approach to be found. This type of system has already been used in US emissions trading to reduce sulphur dioxide and nitrous oxides, the primary components of acid rain, and has been highly successful. The Clean Air Act of 1990 required electrical utilities to lower their emissions of these pollutants by 8.5 million tonnes compared with 1980 levels. Initial estimates in 1989 suggested it would cost $7.4 billion; a report in 1998 based on actual compliance data suggested it had cost less than $1 billion.

The European Trading Scheme (ETS) to reduce greenhouse gases has had mixed success. The ETS includes all 27 EU countries, and all facilities above 20 megawatts, which represents over 40% of the EU gas emissions and includes electricity generation, ferrous metal production, cement production, refineries, pulp, paper, and glass manufacturing. During Phase I, which started in 2005, the price of carbon was very volatile; it rose then fell drastically when verification revealed that too many industrial permits had been issued. Phase II was tougher and reflected some of the lessons learned from Phase I, and it made some progress as there was a real incentive to cut emissions and switch to alternative energy technologies. Phase III will be in line with any post-2012 agreement but must have new targets, and include the chemical and aviation industries. What is required is a global system of cap and trade similar to the ETS, allowing the trading of carbon so that all countries can contract their production.

Global carbon trading will also accelerate the movement of money from the developed to the developing world. This will boost development and provide new consumers and markets, ultimately producing a more equitable distribution of wealth and resources throughout the world. It would also strengthen the world economy, as it would no longer be driven by one or two key nations or trading blocks.

Summary

Global warming can only be solved by binding international agreements to cut global greenhouse gas emissions. The Kyoto Protocol must be recognized as a ground-breaking agreement as over 180 countries signed the global warming pact. The Protocol came into effect on the 16 February 2005, when Russia ratified the treaty, thereby finally meeting the requirement that at least 55 countries, representing more than 55% of the global emissions, signed up to it. The targets for the 37 richest and most developed countries and regions are cuts of 1–8% compared with their 1990 levels. The EU has turned the treaty into law for all member countries, forcing a cut in greenhouse gas emissions of a total 8% on the 1990 level by 2012. At the moment, only a few countries are on target to make their 2012 legally binding cuts and there is no truly effective way of censuring countries that do not make the cuts.

More worrying is the fact that greenhouse gas emissions are now rising faster than the worst-case scenario of the IPCC. To combat this, we need to negotiate a strong post-2012 agreement. This agreement must include developing countries, it must enshrine the principle of contraction and convergence, and it must also protect the rapid development of the very poorest parts of the world. For the post-2012 agreement to work, it must include global carbon trading. This would allow a capitalist system to find the most efficient and cost-effective way of reducing carbon emissions below the defined cap. It would also accelerate the movement of money into the developing world, allowing it to catch up and also stimulate the world economy. Initial signs are very positive for a post-2012 agreement. His Excellency Mr Rachmat Witoelar, chair of the UN Climate Change Conference held in Bali 2007, said:

> The Bali Roadmap [to a post-2012 agreement] is a testament to the remarkable spirit of co-operation that Parties have displayed in these last two weeks. It is also a tribute to the solidarity with which we have come together to address climate change – the defining human development challenge of the 21st century.

The Bali conference is also renowned for the Papua New Guinea delegation telling the US delegation: 'If you're not willing to lead, please get out of the way.' A short time later, the USA reversed its blocking position.

Chapter 8
Solutions

Introduction

The most sensible approach to preventing the worst effects of global warming would be to cut carbon dioxide emissions. Scientists believe a cut of between 60% and 80% is required to prevent the worst effects of global warming (see Chapter 7). But many have argued that the cost of significant cuts in fossil-fuel use would severely affect the global economy, preventing the rapid development of the developing world. It is also clear that current trends of greenhouse gas emissions are now above the worst-case scenarios considered by the 2007 IPCC report. This is primarily due to the rapid development of countries such as China (see Figure 30 for the scale of the recent rise in emissions in China). The Kyoto Protocol, even if it is successful and adhered to, will amount to only a cut of between 1% and 3% for the developed world (Annex 1), while the developing world (non-Annex 1) will continue to increase their emissions. So this chapter examines two types of solution to global warming. First is adaptation, as we already know that there will be climate change even if we reduce our emissions back to 1990 levels. Second is mitigation, which is concerned with reversing this trend and cutting greenhouse gas emissions. This will require regulatory, technological, and economic solutions.

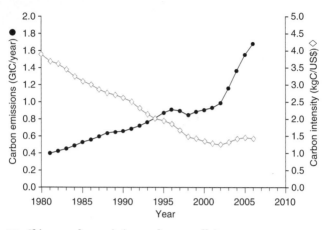

30. Chinese carbon emissions and energy efficiency

Adaptation

There will certainly be climate change. Many countries will be adversely affected in the near future, and nearly all countries will be affected in the next 30 years. So the second major aim of the IPCC is to study and report on the potential sensitivity, adaptability, and vulnerability of each national environment and socioeconomic system, because if we can predict what the impacts of global warming are likely to be, then national governments can take action to mitigate the effects. For example, if flooding is going to become more prevalent in Britain, then damage to property and loss of life can be prevented with strict new laws that limit building on floodplains and vulnerable coasts.

The IPCC believes there are six reasons why we must adapt to climate change: (1) climate change cannot be avoided (see Chapter 4); (2) anticipatory and precautionary adaptation is more effective and less costly than forced last-minute emergency fixes; (3) climate change may be more rapid and more pronounced than current estimates suggest, and unexpected events, as we have seen, are more than just possible; (4) immediate benefits can be gained from better adaptation to climate variability and extreme atmospheric events: for example, with the hurricane risk, strict building laws and better evacuation practices would need to be implemented; (5) immediate benefits can also be gained by removing maladaptive policies and practices, for example, building on floodplains and vulnerable coastlines; and (6) climate change brings opportunities as well as threats. Future benefits can result from climate change. The IPCC has provided many ideas about how one can adapt to climate change; an example is given in Figure 31 of how countries can adapt to predicted sea rise.

The major threat from global warming is its unpredictability (see Chapter 6). Humanity can live in almost any extreme of climate from deserts to the Arctic, but only when we can predict what the extremes of the weather will be. So adaptation is really the key to dealing with the global warming problem, but it must start now, as infrastructure changes can take up to 50 years to implement. For example, if you want to change land-use, for example by building better sea defences or returning farmland back to natural wetlands in a particular area, it can take up to 20 years to research and plan the appropriate measures. It can then take another 10 years for the full consultative and legal processes. It can take another 10 years to implement these changes, and a further decade for the natural restoration to take place (see Figure 32). A good example of this is the Thames Barrier which currently protects London from flooding. It was built in response to the severe flooding in 1953 but did not open officially until 1984, 31 years later.

The other problem is that adaptation requires money to be invested now; many countries just do not have the money, and elsewhere in the world people do not want to pay more taxes to protect themselves in the future as most people live for today. This is, of course, despite the fact that all of the adaptations discussed

Protect

Protect coastal development

Create wetland/mangrove habitat by landfilling and planting

Protect agricultural land

Accommodate

Regulate building development

Strike balance between preservation and development

Switch to aquaculture

Retreat

Establish building setback codes

Allow wetland migration

Relocate agricultural production

Buildings

Wetlands

Crops

31. **Model response strategies for future sea-level rise**

148

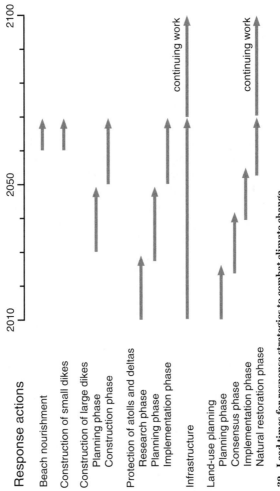

32. Lead times for response strategies to combat climate change

will in the long term save money for the local area, the country, and the world; as a global society we still have a very short-term view, usually measured in a few years between successive governments. Hence the solutions to global warming will have to combine adaptations with the mitigation strategies discussed below. If global carbon trading is adopted in the post-2012 agreement, then this would provide a flow of money to developing countries which could be used to build-in climate change adaptation.

The one thing that every single government can do now is to set up a climate change impact assessment. For example, in the UK there is the UK Climate Impact Programme (<http://www.ukcip.org.uk>) which in January 2009 launched new products, based on the latest IPCC 2007 reports, showing the possible effects of climate change on the UK over the next 100 years. These products are aimed at the UK national and local government, industry, business, the media, and the general public. If every government set up one of these programmes, then at least their citizens would have the information to make informed choices about how their countries should be adapting to climate change.

Mitigation

The idea of cutting global carbon emissions in half in the next 30 years and by up to 80% by the end of the century may sound like fantasy; however, already the United Kingdom and California have made legally binding commitments to reduce carbon emissions by 60% by 2050. Steve Pacala and Robert Socolow, researchers at Princeton University, published a very influential paper in the journal *Science* which makes this challenge seem more achievable. They took the business-as-usual emissions scenario and the desired 450ppm scenario and described the difference between the two as a number of 'wedges'. So on this view, instead of seeing one huge insurmountable problem, really what we are faced with are lots of medium-sized changes which

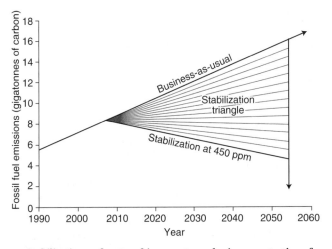

33. Stabilization wedges to achieve an atmospheric concentration of 450ppm carbon dioxide.

add up to the big change (Figure 33). They also provided several examples for the wedges, each of them approximately saving 1 gigatonne of carbon every year, as shown in Table 4. For example, one wedge would be doubling the efficiency of 2 billion cars from 30mpg to 60mpg, which actually is a very achievable aim, as cars have already been built that can easily do 100mpg.

Though Steve Pacala and Robert Socolow provide examples of what we can do to achieve the required cuts in greenhouse gases, each country will have different strengths and weaknesses and can apply the most suitable wedges for them. One of the first measures that all countries, industries, and individuals can take is to be more energy efficient. At the moment, the energy use in an average home in the USA is twice that of the average for California, and California's domestic energy use is twice that of Denmark. So already within the developed world there are huge savings to be made just by improving energy efficiency. It remains a puzzle why industry and business do not improve their energy use, as this can

Table 4. Princeton stabilization wedges

Option	Effort by 2060 each wedge equals 1GtC/yr
Energy efficiency and conservation	
Economy-wide carbon-intensity reduction (emissions/\$GDP)	Increase reduction by additional 0.15% per year (e.g. increase U.S. goal of 1.96% reduction per year to 2.11% per year)
1. Efficient vehicles	Increase fuel economy for 2 billion cars from 30 to 60 mpg
2. Reduced use of vehicles	Decrease car travel for 2 billion 30-mpg cars from 10,000 to 5,000 miles per year
3. Efficient buildings	Cut carbon emissions by one-fourth in buildings and appliances projected for 2060
4. Efficient coal plants	Produce twice today's coal power output at 60% instead of 40% efficiency (compared with 32% today)
Fuel shift	
5. Gas power for coal power	Replace 1400 GW 50%-efficient coal plants with gas plants (four times the current production of gas-based power)
CO_2 Capture and Storage (CCS)	
6. Capture CO_2 at power plant	Introduce CCS at 800 GW coal or 1600 GW natural gas (compared with 1060 GW coal in 1999)
7. Capture CO_2 at H_2 plant	Introduce CCS at plants producing 250 MtH_2 from coal or 500 MtH_2 from natural gas

Table 4. (*Continued*)

Option	Effort by 2060 each wedge equals 1GtC/yr
CO_2 Capture and Storage (CCS)	
8. Capture CO_2 at coal-to-synfuels plants	Introduce CCS at synfuels plants producing 30 million barrels a day from coal (200 times Sasoil) if half of feedstock carbon is available for capture
Geological storage	Create 3500 Sleipners
Nuclear fission	
9. Nuclear power for coal power	Add 700 GW (twice the current capacity)
Renewable electricity and fuels	
10. Wind power for coal power	Add 2 million 1-MW-peak windmills (50 times the current capacity)
11. PV power for coal power	Add 2000 GW-peak PV (700 times the current capacity)
12. Wind H_2 in fuel-cell car for gasoline in hybrid car	Add 4 million 1-MW-peak windmills (100 times the current capacity)
13. Biomass fuel for fossil fuel	Add 100 times the current Brazil or U.S. ethanol production (one-sixth of world cropland)
Forests and agricultural soils	
14. Reduced deforestation, plus reforestation, afforestation and new plantations	Decrease topical deforestation to zero instead of 0.5 GtC/year, and establish 300 Mha of new tree plantations (twice the current rate)
15. Conservation tilage	Apply to all cropland (10 times the current usage)

significantly cut running costs; however, this may be in part capitalists' obsession with turnover and profit. Efficiency gains, however, will ultimately be taken over by increased use. For example, if we did double the efficiency of 2 billion cars, this gain would be wiped out once another 2 billion cars were brought into the world. So one of the most important areas is the production of clean, or carbon-free, energy, discussed below.

Alternative, renewable, or clean energy

We must remember that fossil fuels were an amazing invention, and they have allowed the world to develop at a faster rate than at any time in history. The high standard of living in the developed world is based on cheap and relatively safe fossil fuels. So it is rather naïve to then complain about them or depict them as evil. However, what we do need to do is to replace our reliance on them with carbon-free or so-called renewable or alternative energy sources. This is essential, as the power needs of humanity will continue to expand due to the rapid development of China, India, and other countries. As we have commented, China is opening a new coal-fired power station every four days. This energy expansion is not limited to the developing world: in the UK, there will need to be at least another 20 Petawatts of power generated by 2020. The global demand for fossil fuels is so strong that while writing this book, oil prices peaked at $149 a barrel in July 2008 and are still at $110 a barrel in September 2008 and seem set to continue to be very high for the next few years. There is also concern that we have reached 'peak oil' and that the world is now running out of oil. This does, however, provide two other reasons why countries should adopt a less intensive carbon-energy sector. First, because the era of power from gas and oil will soon be over, due to a combination of huge global demands and dwindling global reserves. Second, countries have in the 21st century become very aware of 'energy security'; most developed countries' economies are heavily reliant on the import of fossil fuels, making them very vulnerable to international blackmail.

Below is a brief discussion of the main alternative energy sources. Straight away you can see how different portfolios fit different countries. For example, the UK has the best wind resource in the whole of Europe, while Saudi Arabia has excellent conditions for solar power.

Low-carbon energy sources

Biomass energy/fuels

Globally biomass energy makes up 10% of the world's energy supply. Unfortunately, this is mainly through simple wood fires in the developing world. 2.4 billion people use biomass fuels to cook and this leads to significant health problems due to indoor pollution. So there is an urgent need to provide clean electricity to help human development. Biofuels, on the other hand, will be essential in the fight to reduce global carbon emissions, as they are an intermediate solution. At the moment, the global economy is based on liquid fossil fuels mainly for the transport sector. We can in the short term use fuels derived from plants as a carbon-neutral way of powering cars, ships, and aeroplanes. There are problems as the production of biofuels will compete with food crops. (See the Transport section below for further details.)

Geothermal

Below our feet, deep within the Earth, is hot molten rock. In some locations, for example in Iceland and Kenya, this hot rock comes very close to the Earth's surface and can be used to heat water to make steam. This is an excellent carbon-free source of energy, because the part of the electricity you generate from the steam you use to pump the water down to the hot rocks. Unfortunately, it is limited by geography. There is, however, another way the warmth of the Earth can be used. All new buildings can have a borehole below them with ground-sourced heat pumps. Cold water is then pumped

---

155

down into these boreholes and the ground warms the water up, cutting the cost of providing hot water to the building.

Hydroenergy

Hydroelectric power is globally an important source of energy. In 2004, it supplied 5% of the world's energy. The majority of the electricity comes from large dam projects. These projects can present major ethical problems as large areas of land must be flooded above the dam, causing mass relocation of people and destruction of the local environment. A dam also slows water flowing down a river and prevents nutrient-rich silt from being deposited lower down. If the river crosses national boundaries, there are potential issues over the rights to water and silt. For example, one of the reasons why Bangladesh is sinking is the lack of silts due to dams on the major rivers in India. There is also a debate about how much greenhouse gas hydroelectric plants save, because even though the production of electricity does not cause any carbon emissions, the rotting vegetation in the area flooded behind the dam does give off significant amounts of methane.

Nuclear fission

Energy is generated when you split heavy atoms such as uranium and this is nuclear fission. It has a very low direct carbon signature, but a significant amount of carbon is generated both mining the uranium and decommissioning the power station. At the moment, 5% of global energy is generated by nuclear power. The new generation of nuclear power stations are extremely efficient, producing nearly 90% of the theoretically possible energy production. Two main disadvantages of nuclear power are the generation of high-level radioactive waste and safety, though improvements in efficiency reduce waste and the new generations of nuclear reactors have state-of-the-art safety precautions built in. There is also the problem that nuclear power in the 'wrong hands' can lead to dangerous nuclear weapons. The advantages of nuclear power, however, are that it is reliable and can react to changing consumer demand throughout the day, and it is technology that is ready to go and already thoroughly tested.

Nuclear fusion

Nuclear fusion is the generation of energy when two smaller atoms are fused together. This is what happens in our Sun and every other star. The idea is that the heavy form of hydrogen which can be found in sea water and lithium can be combined and the only waste product is the non-radioactive gas helium. Using a bath full of water and the lithium from a single laptop battery could provide the energy needs for a person for seven years. The problem, of course, is persuading those two atoms to join together. The Sun does it by subjecting the atoms to incredibly high temperatures and pressures. Some advances have been made at the Joint European Torus (JET) project in the UK, which has produced 16 megawatts of fusion power. The problem is the amount of energy required to generate the huge temperatures in the first place and the difficulty of scaling it up to a power plant size.

Solar heating

The Sun produces a huge amount of heat – the trick is to capture this heat and to use it. On a small scale, houses and other buildings in sunny countries can have solar heating panels on the roofs which heat up water, so people can have carbon-free hot showers and baths. On a large scale, parabolic mirrors are used to focus the solar energy to generate hot liquid (water or oil) to drive turbines to create electricity. The best places to situate solar heat plants are in low-latitude deserts which have very few cloudy days per year. Solar heat plants have been built in California since the 1980s and are now being built in many other countries.

Solar photovoltaic (solar panels)

The individual rays of the Sun hit the solar panel and dislodge electrons inside it, creating an electrical current. The main advantage of solar panels is that you can place them where the energy is needed and avoid all the complicated infrastructure normally required to move electricity around. The scale of projects involving solar panels varies massively from the San Francisco Moscone Conference Centre, which generates 675,000 watts, to Kenya, which has the largest penetration of solar panels of any market but comprising single 18 watt units.

At the moment, the best solar panel is about 17% efficient, which is great compared with photosynthesis which is about 1%, but is a long way off being competitive with other energy sources. Another drawback of current solar panels is that they require silicon, which keeps the cost high. What is needed is a technological breakthrough that would allow solar panels to be made from cheap plastic or some other inexpensive and adaptable material.

Wave

Wave power could be an important source of energy in the future. The concept is simple, to convert the continuous movement of the ocean in the form of waves into electricity. However, this is easier said than done, and experts in the field suggest that wave power is now where solar panel technology was about 20 years ago – lots of catching up required. There are also questions about how much environmental damage may be caused to coastal marine habitats by interrupting or deflecting waves.

Wind

Wind turbines are an efficient means of generating electricity, if they are big enough. The energy generated directly corresponds to the size of the turbine, so the small wind turbines that conscientious people have been putting on the roofs of their houses are almost useless. What you really want are turbines about the size of the Statue of Liberty for maximum effectiveness. It is also more efficient to build wind farms out at sea – more wind, but of course also more costly. The problems with wind turbines are twofold. First, they do not supply a constant source of electricity; if the wind does not blow, then there is no electricity. Second, people do not like them, as they think they are ugly, noisy, and worry about the effects on local natural habitats. All these problems are easy to overcome by situating wind farms in remote locations and out at sea and away from areas of special scientific or natural interest. One study suggests that wind in principle could generate over 125,000 terrawatt-hours, which is five times the current global electricity requirement.

Carbon capture and storage

Removal of carbon dioxide during industrial processes is tricky and costly, because not only does the CO_2 need to be removed, but it must be stored somewhere as well. Removal and storage costs could be somewhere between \$10 and \$50 per tonne CO_2. This would cause a 15% to 100% increase in power production costs. However, recovered CO_2 does not all need to be stored; some may be utilized in enhanced oil recovery, the food industry, chemical manufacturing (producing soda ash, urea, and methanol), and the metal-processing industries. CO_2 can also be applied to the production of construction material, solvents, cleaning compounds and packaging, and in waste-water treatment. But in reality, most of the carbon dioxide captured from industrial processes would have to be stored. It has been estimated that theoretically two-thirds of the CO_2 formed from the combustion of the world's total oil and gas reserves could be stored in the corresponding reservoirs. Other estimates indicate storage of 90–400 gigatonnes in natural gas fields alone and another 90 gigatonnes in aquifers.

Oceans could also be used to dispose of the carbon dioxide. Suggestions have included storage by hydrate dumping – if you mix carbon dioxide and water at high pressure and low temperatures, it creates a solid, or hydrate, which is heavier than the surrounding water and thus drops to the bottom. This hydrate is very similar to the methane hydrates discussed in Chapter 6. Another more recent suggestion is to inject the carbon dioxide half a mile deep into shattered volcanic rocks inbetween giant lava flows. The carbon dioxide will react with the water percolating through the rocks. The acidified water will dissolve metals in the rocks, mainly calcium and aluminium. Once it forms calcium bicarbonate with the calcium, it can no longer bubble out and escape (though if it does escape into the ocean, then bicarbonate is relatively harmless).

The major problem with all of these methods of storage is safety. Carbon dioxide is a very dangerous gas because it is heavier than air and can cause suffocation. An important example of this occurred in 1986, when a tremendous explosion of CO_2 from Lake Nyos, in the west of Cameroon, killed more than 1,700 people and livestock up to 25km away. Though similar disasters had previously occurred, never had so many people and animals been asphyxiated on such a scale in a single brief event. What scientists now believe happened was that dissolved CO_2 from the nearby volcano seeped from springs beneath the lake and was trapped in deep water by the weight of water above. In 1986, there was an avalanche which mixed up the lake waters, resulting in an explosive overturn of the whole lake, and all the trapped carbon dioxide was released in one go, proving that the storage of carbon dioxide is very difficult and potentially lethal. With ocean storage there is the added complication that the ocean circulates, so whatever carbon dioxide you dump, some of it will eventually return. Moreover, scientists are very uncertain about the environmental effects on the ocean ecosystems. However at this very moment huge amounts of carbon dioxide are being pumped around the USA to allow enhanced recovery of oil. There are no reports of any major incidents and engineers working on these pipelines feel that they are much safer than the gas and oil pipe lines which run across most major cities. More globally, however, we currently have no reliable estimates of the amount of CO_2 that could be safely stored.

Transport

I have included a short section on transport here as this is one of the major human contributions to global warming. At the moment, transport accounts for 13% of greenhouse gas emissions globally. In the UK, the carbon emissions from energy production, business, and residential sectors are all going down despite strong annual growth in the UK economy (2.5% per year); but even the UK government admits that transport emissions, mainly from cars, are growing at a formidable rate. A report in 2007 by the UCL Environment Institute suggested that over the next 20 years this growth in car use could wipe out all the cuts in carbon emissions made by the UK since 1990. If we extrapolate this to the rest of the world, we have everyone in the developing world aspiring to have the same standard of living as the West, and that includes at least one car per household and regular holidays by aeroplane.

In respect to cars, there are two possible solutions – biofuels and electricity. Biofuels have been discussed above, and mean that the current infrastructure of providing liquid fuel to cars could be maintained. But as we have seen, biofuels must be carefully produced as they can compete for land-use with food production, can result in tropical deforestation and can still be net emitters of carbon due to transport and production costs. Ultimately, electric cars are the future, because it can be guaranteed that the electricity produced is carbon-neutral. At the moment, we already have hybrid cars which combine a petrol engine with a battery system. This can improve engine efficiency and cut carbon emissions by an average of 50%. It would be an important step forward if all new cars produced had to have this type of system. The next step would be improvement in battery life and the building of infrastructure to allow cars to charge up – just as you charge up your mobile phone at home, you would do the same for your car.

Aeroplanes have become an easy target for climate change campaigners. International flights are not covered by the Kyoto Protocol nor any other international treaty. But at the moment, just 1.6% of global emissions come from aviation. Research is being carried out to see whether a biofuel can be produced that is light enough and powerful enough to replace the traditional air fuel kerosene, though this seems a long way off at the time of writing. Hydrogen is not a solution, because its by-product is water; this is fine on the ground, but high up in the air it produces cirrus clouds which contribute to warming the planet. Since at present there is no real fuel solution for aviation, the airlines are keen to be involved in carbon trading. This way, the airlines can 'off-set' their carbon emissions by ensuring an equivalent amount was saved elsewhere.

Carbon trading

As discussed in Chapter 7, one of the most important tools in Europe to ensure that carbon emissions are lowered is carbon trading. If alternative energy and carbon capture and storage are to be economically viable, then global carbon trading is essential. When Madam Fu Ying, Chinese Ambassador to the UK, visited University College London, she asked me when would it be cost-effective for China to fit carbon capture to their coal-fired power stations. I answered honestly 'never', as the electricity produced will always be more expensive if you have to capture and store the carbon emitted, unless you can then trade the carbon saved on an international stock market to make a profit. The

European Trading Scheme and EU laws are already making renewable sources of energy more competitive. So we must remember that if we really want to switch the global economy away from carbon and on to alternative energy sources and carbon capture and storage, we need a fiscal method to drive the markets. So far, the only approach that seems to have worked within countries and trading blocs is the cap and trade system based on carbon.

Off-setting

One of the most controversial aspects of carbon trading is off-setting. At the moment, this occurs through two systems: the UN Clean Development Mechanism (CDM) and the voluntary markets. The CDM has been described in Chapter 7, and basically UN-certified programmes in developing countries can be funded which make significant greenhouse gas savings. These can include preventing methane release from an abandoned mine, increasing energy efficiency, or solar power or wind power generation. The CDM credits can be bought by countries or through the voluntary market. For example, every time you fly you can buy through a number of companies carbon off-sets equivalent to the carbon emitted on your flight. In the West, a new branding of 'carbon neutral' products has arisen. This seems to encompass anything from television companies such as BSkyB to paper manufacture such as the Arjowiggins Conqueror brand. Off-setting is controversial as it is argued that many of these cuts would have been made anyway, and also it means that companies and people may not be motivated to change their actual behaviours. On a practical level, however, it does offer a way that individuals, companies, and countries can make a difference. It also provides a means of dealing with unavoidable carbon emissions such as from aviation. What does need to happen is for there to be clear global rules on what is and is not an acceptable carbon off-set. There also needs to be a clear verification service to ensure that the carbon saved is really saved.

Geoengineering or technofixes

Geoengineering, also referred to as technofixes or geohacking, always sounds like a Hollywood B-movie. This is because it looks at changing the environment on the planetary scale. Suggestions range from removing carbon dioxide from the atmosphere, either by building artificial trees or by stimulating the oceans to take up more carbon. Other scientists have suggested erecting massive mirrors in space or injecting aerosols into the atmosphere to reduce the amount of sunlight falling on Earth, balancing the heating from global warming. The fundamental problem with all of these approaches is that scientists have no idea what effects they would have. At the moment, scientists are performing one of the largest geoengineering experiments ever undertaken by injecting huge amounts of greenhouse gases into the atmosphere. As this book has shown, we understand that climate change will occur due to this action, but exactly how much and where we do not know. This is equally true of these technofixes – we have no idea if they would work or what unaccounted-for side effects they might have. In many ways, global warming for the Earth can be seen in the same way as illness and the human body: it is always preferable to prevent an illness than to try and cure one, and we all know the potential side effects of drugs, or chemo- or radiation therapy.

One of the famous technofixes was suggested by the late Professor John Martin. He suggested that many of the world's oceans are under-producing. This is because of the lack of vital nutrients, the most important of which is iron, which allows plants to grow in the surface waters. Marine plants need minute quantities of iron and without it they cannot grow. In most oceans enough iron-rich dust gets blown in from the land, but it seems that large areas of the Pacific and Southern Ocean do not receive much dust and thus are barren of iron. So it has been suggested that we could fertilize the ocean with iron to stimulate marine productivity. The extra photosynthesis would convert more surface-water carbon dioxide into organic matter. When the organisms die, the organic matter drops to the bottom of the ocean, taking with it and storing the extra carbon. The reduced surface-water carbon dioxide is replenished by carbon dioxide from the atmosphere. So, in short, fertilizing the world's oceans could help to remove atmospheric carbon dioxide and store it in deep-sea sediments. Experiments at sea have shown that the amount of iron required is huge. Also, as soon as you stop adding the extra iron, most of this stored carbon dioxide is released, as very little organic matter is allowed to escape out of the photic zone.

Another possible solution, advocated in Kunzig and Broecker's book *Fixing Climate*, is the production of artificial trees. Klaus Lackner (a theoretical physicist) and Allen Wright (an engineer), supported by Wally Broecker (a climatologist), have designed CO_2-binding plastic which can scrub carbon dioxide out of the atmosphere. The CO_2 is then released from the plastic and taken away for storage. The problem here is one of scale; tens of millions of these giant artificial trees would be required just to deal with US carbon emissions. We are also left with the problem of how to transport and sequester the carbon safely.

Lastly, on the idea of mirrors to deflect the sunlight. The most sophisticated of these suggestions is from Roger Angel, Director of the Centre for Astronomical Adaptive Optics at the University of Arizona, who suggests a mesh of tiny reflectors to bend some of the light away from the Earth. He himself admits this would be expensive, requiring 16 trillion gossamer-light spacecraft costing at least $1 trillion and taking 30 years to launch. But even then it would not work. Dan Lundt and colleagues at Bristol University showed that the simple sunshade approach does not take us back to a pre-industrial climate. In fact, it takes us to a completely different global climate, with the tropics being 1.5°C colder, the high latitudes would be 1.5°C warmer, and precipitation would drop by 5% globally compared with pre-industrial times. So perhaps we should just stop putting carbon dioxide into the atmosphere.

Summary

If we are to solve global warming, we need to tackle two fundamental principles. The first is to question the currently unsustainable lifestyle that we have in the developed world. If the 21st-century human population of 6–9 billion obtains the same lifestyle as that of the USA, then not only will the requirement for food be greater man supply, but Earth's maximum eco-footprint will also be exceeded. It seems we need at least two planet Earths to support a global population with the same living standards as those in the West. So we need to reduce the energy and material requirements of society, and thus the aspirations of developing countries. It seems that having more stuff does not make us happier, but living longer and having a better quality of life does.

The second principle concerns whether we as a global society are prepared to invest the relatively small amount, about 1–2% of world GDP according to Stern (2007), to off-set a much larger bill in the future. If so, then we have the technology at the moment both to protect our population from climate change and to mitigate the huge predicted emissions of greenhouse gases over the next 100 years. As we have seen, energy efficiency, alternative energy sources, carbon trading, and off-setting all have a role to play. We must also consider 'disruptive technologies', that is, new technologies that we may not yet have even thought of that could change the way we produce or use energy. For example, most of us cannot think of life without a mobile phone or a computer, but this technology has been around for only a few decades; we can quickly become accustomed to change. There are also huge amounts of money to be made from opportunities surrounding changes to our energy use and our personal lifestyles, and as we will see in the next chapter, there may be many win-win situations whereby quality of life can be improved at the same time as we save the planet.

Chapter 9
Visions of a zero-carbon future

In this chapter, I want to provide a vision of the future. Many people now throw around the terms 'zero-carbon cities' and 'zero-carbon economy' but have no idea how to achieve them. What this chapter provides is a look at how our world will change to achieve these goals – because we must realize that our buildings, neighbourhoods, transport networks, and cities *will* all have to change. I am indebted to Professor Yvonne Rydin, Co-Director of the UCL Environment Institute, who has provided the basis for these visions and has very kindly let me steal some of her ideas and expand on them. The following are some suggestions of what the low-carbon world of tomorrow might look like.

Home of the future

- The three-storey town house is part of a group of houses, which collectively make up the GreenHomes Neighbourhood in Anywhere Town in Any Country. They are grouped around a pleasant green space with some play and keep-fit equipment in the centre. There is lots of greenery, some of it acting as sustainable urban drainage systems and the rest as shade from the midday sun. There is a network of local pathways, which are well lit and well used.

- Close by are local shops, a primary school, and a community centre. The community centre notice board is testimony to the number of activities occurring there. Just outside the centre is the express tramway stop, and behind is a small car park with some of the community electric car-share vehicles and communal bicycles.

- The house displays its zero-carbon energy certificate in the hallway but the high levels of insulation in the building fabric are invisible to most visitors. Next to the certificate is the smart meter. This shows the remarkably low levels of electricity usage within the house, thanks to the energy-efficiency measures and the solar water-heating system on the roof. But the meter also shows when electricity is being generated by the household through the photovoltaic cells incorporated into the roof-tiles, window shutters, and other flat surfaces.

- The house is built to deal with the extreme weather predicted for the region: high ceilings, solar shading, and efficient air-conditioning powered by solar panels for the more frequent heat waves; raised ground floor and flood channels in the surrounding area to deal with floods, especially urban flash floods; deep foundations prevent damage to the house from soil shrinkage.

- The house is as water efficient as it is energy efficient. Outside you can see the pipework for the rainwater harvesting system, collecting water into a special tank for feeding through into the house's plumbing system. Water separation is a feature of the house's plumbing, but the household hardly notice this or the water-saving features in the toilets, showers, and sinks.

- There is no garage or off-street parking for the house. Instead, there is a secure cycle store, next to the composting unit. The rest of the household's waste goes into a vacuum waste removal system that also automatically sorts waste for collection and recycling at the community centre.

Office of the future

- FutureOffices are proud of their new headquarters. Approaching it from any of a number of nearby bus-stops, tram-stops, or the train station, visitors are often surprised by its attractive design incorporating greenery at the ground floor, on numerous balconies, and right up to the green roof. The blades of the wind turbines catch the light, giving a clue to how some of the electricity demands of the occupiers are met.

- Less obvious is the system of district heating pipes that connect the office building with other local users – shops, restaurants, the cinema, local health centre, and the college. The mix of users means that the heat demand is more or less balanced over the day and the week. All these users are connected into the area's combined heat and power unit.

- However, FutureOffices Inc. have found the energy demands of its new building are much lower than those of its older buildings. The building's fabric is highly energy efficient but equally as important is the design that maximizes natural daylight while providing shade during the middle of the day, even when the sun is at its hottest. This and the natural internal ventilation system have removed the need for air-conditioning except during extreme heat waves and have made for a much healthier internal environment.

- FutureOffices have made the health of workers a key aspect of the building. The stairs are visible features linking floors, with cafes on mezzanine levels. The stairs are heavily used; the lifts don't stop at every floor, so it is often more convenient to use the stairs. In any case, the lifts are tucked away rather than being the focal point of the lobbies.

- Water-efficiency measures have hugely reduced the water bill. This is despite a dedicated cycle-and-shower unit on the ground floor, with secure cycle storage and changing room facilities.

- Most of the office functions are not at ground-floor level, however, and neither are the core services. The building is not far from the river, and flooding has become more common recently, so the ground floor is flood-proofed to ensure that the next flood will not disrupt business.

Cities of the future

- Our cities have been transformed across the world. Mixed-use developments are situated around vibrant public spaces. These spaces create a strong sense of distinctive place for new developments. The old is integrated into the new, with high-quality urban design.

- Pedestrians are given priority over the car in the planning of cities. There are dedicated routes for trams, guided buses, and cycles linking the different land-uses.

- A mix of micro-generation technologies provide energy for building users. Combined heat and power and district heating schemes are routine for new mixed-use developments, some using renewable fuels. Many of these schemes draw the existing buildings into their scope as well.

- Greenery abounds, on the ground but also on roofs, providing multi-functional spaces for amenity, leisure, natural habitats, and water drainage. Sustainable urban drainage systems are standard, transforming the look of urban areas. Cities are as green and attractive as the countryside.

- Nearby rivers are managed for their landscape, leisure, and nature conservation value. They also form part of urban transport networks, with riverside cycle paths and walkways. Most importantly, the riverbanks and surrounding land absorb rainfall run-off and prevent flooding of built-up areas.

- Such cities encourage people to use their urban areas and to be active within them. Safe, pleasant, and green, cities all over the world contribute to the physical and mental health of their residents.

Transport of the future

- Local travel is now routinely accomplished by public transport, which includes underground and overground trains, buses, trams, and boats. The majority of private cars and taxis are electric. A significant proportion of goods is moved by rail and then efficient electric vans and lorries. Separate cycle lanes and clear, well-lit pedestrians walkways are provided in all urban areas.

- Continental travel has been revolutionized as air traffic has been replaced with Maglev (magnetically levitating) trains travelling at 900km/h (about 600mph) using renewable sources of electricity. These rail networks extend between major cities throughout the world and fast connections allow people to travel across whole continents. The first coast-to-coast train versus plane race in the USA was won by the train; as the walk-on, walk-off train service removed the lengthy delays that occur at the airports.

- Intercontinental travel still uses traditional aeroplanes, but these super-sized commercial jets carry over 1,000 passengers each and are the most efficient ever made. Flights have become very expensive due to the global carbon tax on aviation fuel and thus are always operating at full capacity. They are towed to and from the runway, saving a significant amount of fuel and of course money.

- By the end of the 21st century, resources to fuel the new low-carbon global economy are running low. This is due to both the huge demand as the world rapidly develops and strict new global environmental protection laws. Space exploitation thus becomes cost-effective at the end of the 21st century. Carbon tax breaks on international space launches enable private companies and countries to set up orbiting space stations and the mining of the Moon begins.

Economy of the future

- Carbon Auditors Ltd have just opened their new headquarters in London using all 143 floors of the first zero-carbon skyscraper. This attests to the huge market created in carbon trading since the momentous post-2012 international agreement.

- Renewable and alternative energy companies flourish, replacing the old oil giants as one of the main profit-generating industries in the world. They have been made so profitable by global carbon trading, which is driven by the gradually shrinking global cap on carbon dioxide and other greenhouse gas emissions.

- Technological solutions to both emission reductions and adaptation to climate change have occurred at a fast rate through the 21st century, producing a global developed society unrecognizable from that of a hundred years before. Everything from how plants grow to how we produce electricity has been improved.

- Contrary to the doom merchants, the global economy in the middle of the 21st century is growing at nearly 5% per year – twice the yearly average in the early 21st century. This is due to the increasing flow of money and expertise to the developing world through the post-2012 agreement and global carbon trading. The increased spending power of the developing world has stimulated the global economy, benefiting everyone with improved standards of living. The threat of global warming thus ultimately led to a more equal distribution of wealth across the world and a stronger, faster-growing global economy.

Chapter 10
Conclusion

Global warming is one of the few scientific theories that makes us examine the whole basis of modern society. It is a theory that has politicians arguing, sets nations against each other, queries individual choices of lifestyle, and ultimately asks questions about humanity's relationship with the rest of the planet. There is very little doubt that global warming will change our climate in the next century; our best estimates suggest an average temperature increase of 1.1–6.4°C (probably about 4°C), a sea-level rise in the order of at least half a metre (as long as Greenland and Antarctica do not start to break down), significant changes in weather patterns, and more extreme climate events. This is not the end of the world as envisaged by many environmentalists in the late 1980s and early 1990s, but it does mean a great deal of misery for billions of people.

Global warming is the major challenge for our global society. We should not underestimate the challenge ahead of us. The climate predictions of the IPCC 2007 reports were based on carbon emission scenarios of the next 100 years that were realistic forecasts in 2000. We now know that the economic miracle in China will cause carbon emissions to rise between 11% and 13% between 2000 and 2010, instead of the highest estimate used for Asia by the IPCC of 2.6–4.8%. In addition, the consensus approach used by the IPCC to secure agreement from all parties means it is inherently conservative. We should perhaps therefore view the top estimates of climate change as the more likely to occur; so we are staring down the barrel of a gun, with over 6°C warming by 2100 – and as discussed in Chapter 5, we really do not want to go there. The climate system is not linear, so there will be major tipping points when significant climate changes occur very rapidly. In Figure 34, I have collated the tipping points which colleagues believe are most likely to happen in the near future and will be most devastating. If we cannot reverse the current global emissions trends, all of these tipping points will occur in our future.

Add to this the estimates of top economists that it could cost us up to 20% of everything the world earns in the future to deal with a warmer world. In contrast, it may cost us only 1–2% of what we currently earn to convert our global economy to low-carbon. Even if the cost–benefits are not so great, the ethical case for paying now to prevent the deaths of tens of millions of people and the increase in human misery must be clear.

So what are the solutions to global warming? First, there must be an international political solution; without a post-2012 agreement we are looking at huge increases in global carbon emissions and devastating global warming. Any political agreement will have to include developing countries, and to protect their rapid development, as it is a moral imperative that people in the poorest countries have the right to develop and to obtain the same standards of living we in the West currently enjoy. As far as I can see, the only way to do this is to set up international carbon trading. This way, countries, industry, business, and individuals can reduce their carbon emissions and make money doing so. This is an excellent way for money to flow from richer countries to the poorer countries of the world. Of course, as the poorer countries develop they will have more money to buy low-carbon technology from the richer countries, so continually stimulating the global economy. In addition, it will mean that there will be enough

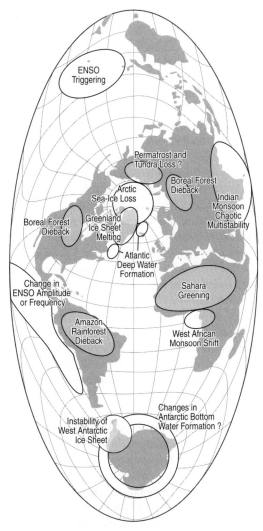

Conclusion

34. Potential climate change tipping points

175

money for developing countries to adapt to the climate changes that will inevitably happen.

Second, we must greatly increase the funding for developing cheap and clean energy production, as all economic development is based on increasing energy usage. This is starting to happen – already, there is US$1 billion investment in clean technology by venture capitalists in Silicon Valley, and this is set to triple into the 2010s. This may sound like a lot of money, but in terms of research and development it is very small. What we really need is a level of funding only ever achieved when a country is at war. The USA has spent over US$1 trillion on the war in Iraq from 2003; just imagine if all that money had been put into developing technology for a zero-carbon world. The International Energy Agency estimates US$20 trillion will be invested in energy over the next 25 years – what we must do is to ensure that it is not in fossil fuels. But even if renewable energy technology does become available, there is no guarantee that it would be made affordable to all nations, since we live in a world where even life-saving drugs are costed to achieve maximum profit. Nor is there any guarantee that if we had unlimited free energy it would prevent us from continuing to abuse the planet: Paul Ehrlich at Stanford University, commenting on the possibility of unlimited clean energy from cold fusion, suggested it would be 'like giving a machine gun to an idiot child'.

We must not pin all our hopes on global politics and clean energy technology, so we must prepare for the worst and adapt. If implemented now, a lot of the costs and damage that could be caused by changing climate can be mitigated. This requires nations and regions to plan for the next 50 years, something that most societies are unable to do because of the very short-term nature of politics. So global warming challenges the very way we organize our society. Not only does it challenge the concept of the nation-state versus global responsibility, but the short-term vision of our political leaders. To answer the question of what we can do

35. Is global warming all bad?

about global warming, we must change some of the basic rules of
our society to allow us to adopt a much more global and long-term
approach.

I leave you with thoughts of redesigning our global community
and with the slogan my wife dreamt up for the UCL Environment
Institute, because we really do need . . .

Cool solutions for a hotter world.

Further reading

History of climate change

J. Corfee-Morlot, et al., Climate Science in the Public Sphere, *Philosophical Transactions A of the Royal Society*, 365/1860 (2007): 2741–2776.

J. K. Leggett, *The Carbon War: Global Warming and the End of the Oil Era* (Routledge, 2001).

—— *Half-Gone: Oil, Gas, Hot Air and the Global Energy Crisis* (Portobello, 2006).

S. R. Weart, *The Discovery of Global Warming, New Histories of Science, Technology, and Medicine* (Harvard University Press, 2003).

Science

R. W. Battarbee and H. A. Binney (eds), Natural climate variability and global warming: A Holocene perspective (10 key papers) (Wiley-Blackwell, 2008).

J. Gribbin, *Hothouse Earth: The Greenhouse Effect and Gaia* (Grove Weidenfeld, 1990).

D. Harvey, *Global Warming: The Hard Science* (Prentice Hall, 2000).

J. T. Houghton, Global Warming: The Complete Briefing, 3rd edn. (Cambridge University Press, 2004).

J. C. R. Hunt, M. Maslin, P. Backlund, T. Killeen, and H. J. Schellnhuber (eds.), 'Climate Change and Urban Areas (nine key

papers)', *Philosophical Transactions of the Royal Society of London*,
series A, 365/1860 (2007): 2613–2776.

IPCC, *Climate Change 2007: The Physical Science Basis*, Contribution
of Working Group I to the Fourth Assessment Report of the
Intergovernmental Panel on Climate Change, ed. S. Solomon et al.
(Cambridge University Press, 2007).

J. H. Lawton, J. Marotzke, R. March, and I. N. McCave (eds.), 'Abrupt
Climate Change: Evidence, Mechanism and Implications (fourteen
key papers)', *Philosophical Transactions of the Royal Society of
London*, series A, 361/1810 (2003): 1827–2078.

National Research Council, *Abrupt Climate Change: Inevitable
Surprises* (National Academy Press, 2002).

Impact assessments

IPCC, *Climate Change 2007: Impacts, Adaptation, and Vulnerability*,
Contribution of Working Group II to the Fourth Assessment
Report of the Intergovernmental Panel on Climate Change, ed.
Parry et al. (Cambridge University Press, 2007).

National Assessment Synthesis Team, *Climate Change Impacts on the
United States—Overview Report* (Cambridge University Press,
2000).

M. Parry, J. Paluyokof, C. Hanson, and J. Lowe, 'Squaring Up to
Reality', *Nature*, reports on climate change, 2 (June 2008): 1–3.

Policy

IPCC, *Climate Change 2007: Mitigation of Climate Change*,
Contribution of Working Group III to the Fourth Assessment
Report of the Intergovernmental Panel on Climate Change, ed.
B. Metz et al. (Cambridge University Press, 2007).

S. Labatt and R. R. White, *Carbon Finance* (Wiley, 2007).

M. Maslin et al., *Audit of UK Greenhouse Gas Emissions to 2020: Will
Current Government Policies Achieve Significant Reductions?*, UCL
Environment Institute: Environment Policy Report Number
2007:01, p. 61. (<http://www.ucl.ac.uk/environment-institute/
Publications/UCLEI-report.pdf>).

R. Pielke Jr, T. Wigley, and C. Green, 'Dangerous Assumptions',
Nature, 452 (April 2008): 531–2.

N. Stern, *The Economics of Climate Change: The Stern Review* (Cambridge University Press, 2007).

H. J. Schellnhuber et al. *Avoiding Dangerous Climate Change* (Cambridge University Press, 2006).

Solutions

T. Blair and The Climate Group, *Breaking the Climate Deadlock: A Global Deal for Our Low-Carbon Future*, Report submitted to the G8 Hokkaido Toyako Summit (June 2008), downloadable from http://tonyblairoffice.org/2008/03/tony-blair-launches-climate-ch.html

R. Gelbspan, *Boiling Point* (Basic Books, 2005).

M. Hillman, *How We Can Save the Planet* (Penguin Books, 2004).

R. Kunzig and W. Broecker, *Fixing Climate* (GreenProfile, in association with Sort of Books, 2008).

A. Meyer, *Contraction and Convergence: The Global Solution to Climate Change* (Green Books, 2000).

G. Monbiot, *Heat* (Allen Lane, Penguin Group, 2006).

OECD, Bridge over troubled water: Linking climate change and development (OECD Publishing, 2005).

S. Roaf, D. Crichton, and F. Nicol, *Adapting Building and Cities for Climate Change* (Elsevier, 2005).

J. Sachs, *The End of Poverty* (Penguin, 2005).

O. Tickell, *Kyoto2: How to Manage the Global Greenhouse* (Zed Books, 2008).

G. Walker and D. King, *The Hot Topic* (Bloomsbury, 2008).

General reading

J. Adams, *Risk* (UCL Press, 1995).

B. Lomborg, *The Skeptical Environmentalist: Measuring the Real State of the World* (Cambridge University Press, 2001).

R. Henson, *The Rough Guide to Climate Change* (Rough Guides, 2006).

M. Lynas, *Six Degrees: Our Future on a Hotter Planet* (Fourth Estate, 2007).

B. McGuire, *Seven Years to Save the Planet: The Questions and Answers* (Weidenfeld & Nicolson, 2008).

R. C. L. Wilson, S. A. Drury, and J. L. Chapman, *The Great Ice Age: Climate Change and Life* (Routledge, 2003).

Fiction inspired by climate change

N. Astley (ed.), *Earth Shattering: Ecopoems* (Bloodaxe Books, 2007).

J. Cowley (ed.), *Granta 102: The New Nature Writing* (Granta: Magazine of New Writing, 2008).

K. Evans, *Funny Weather* (Myriad Editions, 2006).

J. Griffiths, *WILD – An Elemental Journey* (Penguin Books, 2008).

P. F. Hamilton, *Mindstar Rising* (Pan Books, 1993).

K. S. Robinson, *Forty Signs of Rain* (HarperCollins, 2004).

J. Winterson, *The Stone Gods* (Hamish Hamilton, 2007).

Index

Index

Expand your collection of
VERY SHORT INTRODUCTIONS